Urban Finance Under Siege

Those of the street   1/1   D. Kinsey 1993

Urban Finance Under Siege

Thomas R. Swartz
Frank J. Bonello

Editors

M. E. Sharpe Inc.
Armonk, New York
London, England

Library of Congress Cataloging-in-Publication Data

Urban finance under siege / Thomas R. Swartz and
Frank J. Bonello, editors.
p. cm.
Includes bibliographical references and index.
ISBN 1–56324–224–9 (cloth).—ISBN 1–56324–225–7 (pbk.)
1. Municipal finance—United States. 2. Municipal revenue—
United States. 3. Urban policy—United States.
I. Swartz, Thomas R.
II. Bonello, Frank J.
HJ9145.U62 1993
336′.01473—dc20
92–40741
CIP

Printed in the United States of America

The paper used in this publication meets the minimum
requirements of American National Standard for Information
Sciences—Permanence of Paper for Printed Library Materials,
ANSI Z39.48–1984.

∞

MV (c)   10 9 8 7 6 5 4 3 2 1
MV (p)   10 9 8 7 6 5 4 3 2 1

To

Theodore M. Hesburgh, CSC
President Emeritus, University of Notre Dame

Contents

List of Figures and Tables

Preface

The responsibility to provide basic government services—elementary and secondary education, public safety, streets and highways, public assistance, general government—has experienced several dramatic reversals over the past forty years. In the immediate post–World War II period, local governments were nearly totally responsible for these expenditures, which they supported with revenues from the then powerful property tax. However, as society became increasingly aware of the disparities in the fiscal capacity of local governments, fiscal responsibility was "assumed" by higher levels of government: state and federal government.

The process of leveling the playing field for local governments continued through most of the 1960s and 1970s. By the end of the 1970s, however, public policy once again experienced a reversal. We entered the age of devolution, in which local governments were expected to pay their own way. A libertarian-like philosophy of government developed, which demanded that individuals take responsibility for their own actions or inactions and also expected local governments to fend for themselves.

Unfortunately, the once dominant property tax had become a slender profile of its former self. Over time its tax base had been systematically eroded to make way for green space, public buildings, new streets and expressways, and innumerable other tax-exempt activities. More recently, this same tax base has suffered yet another direct assault: the sharp decline in residential and commercial values that has occurred in many communities, particularly on our coasts.

Thus at the very moment that higher levels of government mandate that local governments take fiscal responsibility for the provision of basic government services, the revenue capacity of their principal tax is called into question. How narrow is the property tax base? Will the decline in residential and commercial property values translate into a sharp drop in assessed value in the foreseeable future? What are the other sources of revenue that local governments can turn to in their efforts to underwrite the costs of their new expenditure obligations? As we approach the twenty-first century, can we legitimately expect local governments, particularly those that are fiscally stressed, to overcome somehow the deep-seated national malaise that is associated with our loss of stature in the world economy? Or, alternatively, have the electronic and print media and some professional urbanologists overstated the problems faced by urban America?

These and many other related questions are considered in the essays that follow. Five of the nation's most respected scholars of local government finance visited us here at Notre Dame to examine the root causes of fiscal stress endured by many U.S. cities, the effectiveness of the policy instruments that have been fashioned to address the plight of urban areas, and the prognosis for the future. The willingness of our participants to reorder their priorities to make room for this project on their over-committed calendars testifies to the urgency of the problems confronted by U.S. cities, large and small. If we as a society are to remain a real presence in the modern-day world, we cannot ignore the warning signs found in the pages that follow. We cannot afford a policy of benign neglect.

This project was made possible by the active support of the Institute for Scholarship in the Liberal Arts, the Department of Economics, and a generous grant from the Paul M. and Barbara Henkels Visiting Scholars series at the University of Notre Dame.

T. R. Swartz
F. J. Bonello
1993

Urban Finance Under Siege

1

Rethinking Urban Finance in America

Thomas R. Swartz

The New Urban Poverty

We are quick to believe that the problems we face as a society are the worst problems our society has ever faced. For the poor trapped in many of our cities, this may be true. These cities are plagued by unemployment rates, particularly among African-Americans, Hispanics, and teenagers, that rival the experiences of the 1930s; a decaying stock of affordable houses that has not been systematically replenished by public housing authorities; an education system that "fails" those who are most in need of its benefits; and infrastructure that has been left to crumble because funds are needed to plug gaping holes in municipal budgets rather than holes in water mains, sewer lines, or, as in the case of Chicago, an abandoned underground access system. Unfortunately, this short list of problems fails to capture the real poverty of urban poverty: the fatalism of urban gangs; the explosion of teenage pregnancies; the devastating effects of crack, coke, and alcohol; the horror of AIDS as it spreads unabated; and the sense of isolation and rejection as the affluent, mostly suburban community turns its back on those who are inescapably caught in this whirlpool of decline.

The Old Urban Poverty

The horror faced by today's urban poor, however, obscures the fact that cities have always been harsh places to live if you were poor. Capture in your mind's eye a picture of the city at the turn of the century. There were unpaved or crudely paved streets crowded with traffic—a mixture of horse-drawn wagons and primitive gas-powered cars and trucks, each emitting its own pollution, the former biodegradable perhaps but nevertheless an unpleasant pollutant. Raw sewage flowed in open gutters downhill toward bodies of water that often represented the city's transportation system and only source of potable water. Heavy black smoke hung low in the sky, as both homes and factories were fueled by coal. Cities were loud, dirty, crude, unsafe, eerie, and unpredictable, particularly if you wandered into the areas where the poorest of the poor lived in tenements and other makeshift homes.

If you had money, however, you didn't have to endure the hardships of the city. At least you didn't have to live in the midst of those problems, even if you had to spend your workdays there. You could move to the end of the trolley line. You could move to a converted farmhouse on the edge of the city. Or you could move to the top of "Knob Hill" and get above the pollution while your wastewater ran downhill to those less fortunate than you. In brief, if you had the wherewithal you could separate yourself from the problems of the city. In days gone by, just as today, you could economically isolate yourself from an undesirable situation—you could buy your way out.

The Tiebout Effect

The motivation to flee things that we find to be "undesirable" is rooted in economics and was first discussed by Charles Tiebout (Tiebout 1956). We respond to what we perceive to be negative externalities or negative spillover effects from our neighbors. Although we try to control the actions of our neighbors both within the law with local ordinances or zoning restrictions and federal or state statutes, and outside the law with intimidation and social pressure, sometimes this simply does not work. That is, third parties over whom we have no control can directly and significantly affect us. If my neighbor lets her house fall into disrepair, the value of her property falls, but in addition I pay part of the cost of her decision or lack of action: the value of my house falls. If I am surrounded by negative externalities—houses in disrepair, congested streets, drug dealers, prostitutes, dirty book stores, rats in the alleyways—in an effort to minimize my loss I may be forced to move.

There are two obvious implications of this. First, not everyone has the luxury of fleeing negative externalities. The aged may be too deeply rooted in their neighborhoods or too dependent upon urban public and private services to pick up and escape, while the poor simply do not have the wherewithal to move. Mobility is a privilege, therefore, that the market reserves for a few: primarily the affluent members of society.

The second implication is less obvious and ultimately more devastating for urban finance. It concerns the terminus of the moves. If our mobile affluent move within the civil boundaries of the city, the municipal tax authority still has access to their taxpaying capacity; if our affluent move beyond the civil boundaries, however, it becomes much more difficult for the city to claw-back tax revenue from them even though these individuals may still work within the city and continue to benefit from the multitude of services provided by the city. In the words of the late Father Geno Baroni—a community activist of the 1960s and 1970s—if we don't stop the outmigration of the rich from the city proper, "cities will become *black, brown, and broke.*"

The Problem Begins

That is exactly what began to happen in the mid 1950s. Prior to that time, when the affluent moved away from what they found to be negative externalities, they remained in the city. Sometime in the 1950s this pattern changed. Those who moved to avoid negative externalities, moved outside of the taxing authority of the city. They moved to suburbia. As Katharine Lyall explains in the next chapter of this book, this outmigration has potentially devastating effects for our cities.

Because of these changing demographics, the very character of our cities changed in the 1950s and 1960s. In the presence of great wealth, large, rapidly growing pockets of urban poverty began to appear. In addition to rural poverty, America now had urban poverty that was spreading at an alarming rate. City after city, particularly in the Northeast Corridor and in the Great Lakes Region, began to experience fiscal stress as the young and the affluent fled to the suburban rings that encircled our cities. As fewer and fewer wealthy taxpayers were forced to support the ongoing expenses of the city, urban tax rates had to rise. As tax differentials between cities and the suburban rings that surrounded them grew, more affluent families were pulled away from their urban roots.

Other wealthy urbanites were pushed out of cities. These were families in search of superior public goods and services: good schools, safe streets, green parks, less congestion, and so on. That is, as the composition of the urban population changed and poor people became a larger percentage of the total population, the tax base narrowed. (See Dick Netzer's discussion of this in chapter 3.) City officials believed they had little choice but to eliminate public spending on luxury items: parks, zoos, libraries, special education programs for the gifted, summer recreation and crafts programs, improvements in golf courses and swimming pools. These "frills" were replaced by increased expenditures on the urban safety net that had to protect an increasing number of families from abject poverty.

The consequence is obvious. Since the wealthy had to pay a higher tax price for a bundle of public goods and services that they had little or no use for—public housing, food stamps and Medicaid, general welfare, public defenders—in the words of Charles Tiebout, they "voted with their feet." They did exactly what economists would expect: they sought out and found a bundle of public goods and services that fit their needs at a tax price they were willing to pay. These were the goods and services provided by suburban communities.

Unfortunately, this problem was not self-correcting. Indeed, in the short term the prognosis was grim. As more and more of our rich left the city, they took with them their taxpaying power and their positive externalities. They left behind a community with an eroding tax base and a growing expenditure need. In recognition of this, federal and state governments stepped in to halt the downward spiral.

Leveling the Playing Field

Federal grants-in-aid to state and local governments increased sharply.[1] In the 1950s, federal support represented little more than 10 percent of state and local government spending. Throughout the 1960s and most of the 1970s these grants steadily rose, as public policy explicitly attempted to level the playing field for state and local governments. Indeed, federal programs designed to impact directly impoverished areas sprouted like mushrooms after a rainstorm. Kennedy's New Frontier, Johnson's Great Society, and Nixon's New Federalism gave us Medicare/Medicaid, the Economic Opportunity Act, Community Development Block Grants, General Revenue Sharing, Urban Development Action grants, the Comprehensive Employment and Training Act, Titles I and II of the Elementary and Secondary Education Act, the Economic Development Administration— the list goes on and on. By 1978, the peak year for federal support of lower levels of governments, federal grants supported 25.3 percent of state and local spending.

Competitive Federalism

As Table 1.1 suggests, these lower levels of government were in for a rude awakening. Beginning with the Carter administration, then pursued with a vengeance by the Reagan and Bush administrations, the federal government changed policy direction. Instead of reducing the apparent differences among cities and among states, the new policy heightened them. This was the age of "competitive federalism," in which the laws of the market were

Table 1.1

Intergovernmental Fiscal Flows, 1954–89

Federal Intergovernmental Expenditures to State and Local Governments (Annual Percentage Change)

Years	Total	Education	Highways	Public Welfare	Housing and Urban Development	General Revenue Sharing*	All Others
1954–64	13.0	11.2	21.2	7.5	20.1	-	13.0
1964–74	15.6	18.5	2.3	15.8	15.5	-	19.8
1974–79	14.8	8.7	9.8	12.9	21.8	2.3	25.9
1980–84	3.3	3.8	8.0	11.5	8.9	-7.2	-5.7
1985–89	5.2	10.0	6.4	7.1	6.4	-22.4	1.9

State Intergovernmental Expenditures to Local Governments (Annual Percentage Change)

Years	Total	Education	Highways	Public Welfare	General Support	All Others
1954–64	8.6	10.1	5.8	7.7	5.8	8.5
1964–74	13.2	13.8	7.1	12.6	4.6	8.2
1974–79	10.6	11.3	5.3	4.8	11.4	19.2
1980–84	7.5	7.9	6.5	6.9	5.5	8.5
1985–89	9.2	9.2	5.7	10.7	8.0	11.9

Source: *Significant Features of Fiscal Federalism, 1991*, Volume 2 (Washington, D.C.: Advisory Commission on Intergovernmental Relations, October 1991), Tables 25 and 29.
*This program was eliminated for state governments in 1980 and for local governments in 1986.

forced upon the public domain. General Revenue Sharing, Nixon's domestic gemstone, which provided unencumbered money to state and local governments, was gutted in the early 1980s and eliminated in 1986. Grants for housing and urban development were slashed—in some years of the 1980s no new moneys were allocated for public housing. Public welfare grants were cut, highway support was reduced, and even popular education grants were cut. Thus, whereas federal grants grew annually by double-digit percentages under Kennedy, Johnson, and Nixon—13 percent annually in the 1954–64 period, 15.6 percent annually in the 1964–74 period, and 14.8 percent annually in the 1974–79 period—they grew by only 3.3 percent annually in the 1980–84 period and 5.2 percent annually in the 1985–89 period. Since inflation averaged 4 percent per year throughout most of this period, federal support was systematically choked off.

The problems for local governments didn't end there. State governments by and large tried to make up the difference for their local governments; but as Table 1.1 indicates, in most categories of support they were waging an uphill battle. Their own support of local governments grew, but annually the rate of growth in the 1980s lagged behind the growth rate of state grants of the 1960s and 1970s.

State efforts to bail their local governments out of the consequence of changing federal priorities is better seen in Figure 1.1, which provides a historical profile of state aid relative to the revenues generated by local governments from their own sources. Shortly after federal support of state and local government programs began to fall, state governments began to withdraw their support of local programs. State aid as a percent of local government's own revenue increased steadily throughout the late 1960s and 1970s, rising from the low 40 percent range in the 1950s and early 1960s to a high of 63.5 percent in 1979. One year after the federal government reined in its grants-in-aid, state governments—perhaps feeling the loss of these federal dollars—began to rein in their support of local programs.

State support fell sharply throughout the early 1980s. This

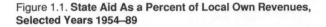

Figure 1.1. **State Aid As a Percent of Local Own Revenues,
Selected Years 1954–89**

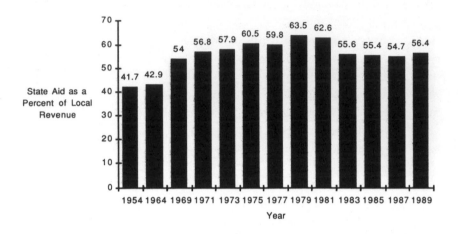

support now appears to have settled in at a rate in the mid–50
percent range. Given the sagging state of the national economy,
the effects of state and local expenditure cuts, and the general
"no new taxes" mood that has paralyzed the American body
politic, there is little reason to expect a change in this trend.
Indeed, if the United States does experience a triple-dip recession, there is every reason to expect further withdrawal of state
support of local government spending.

The Devolution of Governmental Responsibility

The facts are starkly obvious for all to see: Local governments will
soon assume the expenditure responsibility for basic government that
they provided in the pre-Kennedy-Johnson years. Local governments
will, in the words of John Shannon, have to "fend for themselves."[2]

The question we must ask is: *How will local governments
respond to this new challenge?* The short answer to this question
is that they will return to what has always been the backbone of
local government finance: the property tax.

Table 1.2

Percentage Distribution of Local Government General Revenue, Selected Years 1948–89

Years	1948	1958	1968	1978	1979	1980	1981	1982	1983	1984	1985	1986	1987	1988	1989
Own Source Taxes															
• Property	51.4	48.7	42.5	32.9	29.5	28.2	28.0	28.1	28.8	28.6	28.2	28.2	28.4	29.3	29.3
• General and Selective Sales	3.5	3.9	3.1	4.8	5.0	5.2	5.1	5.3	5.5	5.7	5.9	5.9	6.0	6.0	5.9
• Individual*	0.4	0.8	1.7	2.1	2.0	2.1	2.2	2.2	2.2	2.2	2.3	2.2	2.4	2.4	1.9
Charges and Miscellaneous	11.2	14.0	15.4	15.6	17.3	18.8	19.8	21.6	22.1	22.6	25.0	23.2	23.4	23.0	23.2
Intergovernmental	30.8	30.2	35.3	43.2	44.7	44.1	43.3	41.5	40.0	39.2	39.0	38.7	38.1	37.5	37.4
Other	2.7	2.4	2.1	1.5	1.5	1.6	1.6	1.4	1.5	1.6	1.6	1.7	1.8	1.8	2.3

Source: Significant Features of Fiscal Federalism, 1991, Volume 2 (Washington, D.C.: Advisory Commission on Intergovernmental Relations, October 1991), Tables 74 and 80.

*This table excludes corporate income tax revenue since nearly all of the local corporate income taxes are raised in New York City and the District of Columbia. In 1989, total local corporate taxes were approximately $2,060 million, while total local individual income taxes were $8,988 million.

The Reemergence of the Property Tax

The shifting pattern that places a greater dependence on the property tax is not obvious in the national data. Table 1.2 suggests that the importance of property taxation has remained constant throughout most of the 1980s, hovering at about 28 or 29 percent of local government general revenue. This implies that the dependence on the property tax, which fell markedly in the post–World War II period, has stabilized. There is certainly no indication in the undisaggregated national data that there has been a radical change in this established pattern.

These national averages, however, obscure the fact that the local governments most impacted by federal and state reductions in grants have responded differently than the states that have not suffered this fiscal stress. That is, a careful disaggregation of the data that identifies those states whose local governments have experienced the largest relative loss in federal and state support reveals that property tax dependence in those states is on the rise.

That story is told in Table 1.3. Here the ten states that experienced the sharpest reductions in federal and state grants are isolated and analyzed separately. These ten states are believed to be most impacted by the changing fiscal federalism that occurred in the 1978–87 ten-year interval. They were identified by an "Index of Change in Fiscal Federalism," which in simple terms is the state-by-state sum of the percentage change in federal grants to state and local governments plus the percentage change in state grants to their local governments during the 1978–87 period. It is expected that by identifying the ten states that are the objective losers in this devolutionary process, we can examine how they responded to these unhappy circumstances.

Before we move on to a discussion of Table 1.3, however, we should note that our "index of change"—or, the percentage change in local grant support—reflects the fact that without exception federal grants to state and local governments fell in all states between 1978 and 1989. When this is coupled with the decline in state grants to their local governments—approximately

Table 1.3

Changes in Local Government Grant and Tax Patterns 1978–89, Measured As a Percentage of Local Total Revenue

| | Percent Change in Local Grants | Grants As a Percent of Total Revenue | | Sales Tax As Percent of Total Revenue | | Income Tax As Percent of Total Revenue | | Other Taxes As Percent of Total Revenue | | Charges & Miscellaneous As Percent of Total Revenue | | | | Property Tax As Percent of Total Revenue | |
| | | | | | | | | | | Charges/Miscellaneous | | Charges/Miscellaneous only | | | |
	1978–89	1978	1989	1978	1989	1978	1989	1978	1989	1978	1989	1978	1989	1978	1989
Hawaii	−44.4	33.3	21.3	—	—	—	—	10.4	12.5	10.8	18.5	9.7	9.1	40.5	47.7
New Hampshire	−37.9	25.3	15.7	—	—	—	—	1.2	0.5	10.2	13.0	9.9	8.8	63.3	70.8
Louisiana	−27.3	49.9	36.3	14.8	16.4	—	—	2.7	3.2	18.4	27.7	16.9	16.6	14.3	16.5
Texas	−27.1	37.8	27.1	3.9	4.9	—	—	2.5	2.8	19.8	28.1	17.2	15.7	36.0	37.1
Oregon	−26.0	41.9	31.0	—	—	—	—	3.6	5.0	16.9	22.1	16.0	14.1	37.5	41.9
Florida	−25.2	43.3	32.4	—	∨	—	—	5.0	6.5	24.8	33.5	21.8	18.7	26.8	27.5
Oklahoma	−21.1	47.0	37.1	9.6	11.8	—	—	1.9	1.9	19.2	28.5	17.1	18.6	22.2	20.5
New York	−20.7	44.9	35.6	6.7	8.2	5.0	7.5*	2.4	4.0	11.2	16.1	10.5	10.7	29.9	28.5
Colorado	−20.7	36.6	29.0	9.6	11.7	—	—	2.6	2.5	17.5	24.8	15.8	14.0	33.7	31.9
Mississippi	−17.0	54.0	44.8	—	∨	—	—	1.2	1.3	24.8	33.8	22.7	25.8	20.1	20.1
10-State average	−26.0	41.9	31.0	4.6	5.3	0.5	0.7	3.6	4.0	17.4	24.6	18.8	15.2	32.4	34.3
(change, 10-State)		(−10.9)		(+0.7)		(+0.25)		(+0.4)		(+7.2)		(−0.6)		(+1.9)	
U.S. Average	−13.4	43.2	37.4	3.2	4.1	2.1	2.3	3.1	3.7	15.6	23.2	14.2	14.1	32.9	29.3
(change, U.S.)		(−5.8)		(+0.9)		(+0.2)		(+0.6)		(+7.6)		(−0.1)		(−3.6)	

Source: Significant Features of Fiscal Federalism 1979/80, Volume 2, Table 57 and *1991*, Volume 2, Table 92 (Washington, D.C.: Advisory Commission on Intergovernmental Relations, October 1980 and October 1991); and T.R. Swartz, "The Cost of the New System of Fiscal Federalism in the U.S.," an unpublished paper prepared for an international symposium on fiscal federalism (Seefeld/Tyrol, Austria: Institut für Finanzwissenschaft der Universität Innsbruck. March 16–17. 1990).
*Excludes local corporate income taxes.

two-thirds of the states reduced their per capita grants—the states whose local governments are the most severely affected clearly emerge. While the local governments in the average state experienced a 13.4 percent reduction in support, our subset of ten states lost an average of 26 percent. This group was led by Hawaii— 44.4 percent—and concluded by Mississippi, whose local governments lost 17.0 percent.

We should also note that one striking feature of this group of states is that they are drawn from nearly every region of the country. They stretch from New York and New Hampshire in the Northeast to Hawaii in the Far West and from Oregon in the Northwest to Florida in the Southeast. There are sunbelt states, mountain states, border states, and southwestern states. The only regions not represented among the ten are the Great Lakes and the Plains states. Thus, there should be no obvious regional bias that would shape how they responded to the deep cuts in federal and state grants-in-aid.

Table 1.3 focuses solely on the tax patterns of these ten states. The table is constructed so as to concentrate upon the *relative* importance of different taxes within these states at the end of the "golden years" for local governments, when federal and state governments were most aggressive in their attempts to level the playing field, and these same taxes twelve years later. Consequently, the table is stated in percentage terms.

What is implied here is that the local governments of the heavily impacted states have adjusted to the drop in grants-in-aid by increasing their dependency on all available revenue sources: sales taxes (+0.7 percent), income taxes (+0.25 percent), other taxes (+0.4 percent), charges and miscellaneous revenues (+7.2 percent), and property taxes (+1.9 percent). The latter two categories deserve special attention.

For those of us who have watched the much unaligned property tax slide from its dominant place in local government finance to what appeared to be eventual obscurity, the implications found in Table 1.3 are intriguing: the property tax is on its way back. In 1978, before the federal and state withdrawal of support, property taxes represented 32.4 percent of the revenues of local governments in our ten states. At that time, these ten states were representative of the nation at large; the typical state averaged 32.9 percent dependency on the property tax. This in itself is not surprising, since, as noted earlier, these states are geographically dispersed across the country.

What is surprising is that over the next eleven years, these ten states do not follow the national trend away from the property tax. In fact, in seven of the ten states, property taxes increase and in some cases increase substantially. For example, property taxes as a percent of own revenue rise from 63.3 percent to 70.8 percent in New Hampshire, and from 40.5 percent to 47.7 percent in Hawaii. Even in the three states that follow the national trend, the decrease in property tax dependency is moderate: 29.9 to 28.5 percent in New York, 33.7 to 31.9 percent in Colorado, and 22.5 to 20.5 percent in Oklahoma.

Another way to look at this pattern is to examine the property tax levy itself. It is well established that this tax is far and away the most productive tax instrument in the local government fiscal arsenal. Although it no longer generates nine-tenths of local government tax revenue as it did in the immediate post–World War II period, it continued to generate three-fourths of that revenue throughout the 1980s. What is of interest for our purposes is that the nominal property tax levy for the country as a whole increased by 114 percent in the 1978–89 period. The property levy in our subset of ten states increased by 152 percent during the same period. Is this a precursor of the future? That is, will other states allow their local governments to increase their property taxes to pay for our new "decentralized" system of fiscal federalism? I am inclined to say yes.

Band-aid Solutions

We can hardly move away from Table 1.3 without examining the other set of startling statistics: "Charges and Miscellaneous Revenues." For the country as a whole, these have risen by 7.6 percentage points in the 1978–89 period. The grant-starved states have experienced a slightly smaller increase (7.2 percent) in this category, which may suggest that there is some finite limit for this source of revenue. Even if that is true, we can hardly ignore this nontax revenue source that now rivals the highly productive property tax.

Unfortunately, this particular shift in revenue patterns is difficult to interpret. The category "current charges and miscellaneous revenue" is simply too inclusive to analyze with the data that are currently published. However, by breaking out "current charges" from the miscellaneous revenues, one misconception can be eliminated. That is the relative importance of current charges. It was assumed by many that those charges would prove to be the principal source of new revenue for states heavily impacted by the reduction in intergovernmental revenues. In reality, current charges have not changed in any significant way for either our ten-state group or the country at large.

Thus, we are left to struggle with the vagueness of the "miscellaneous revenue" category and the implications of its sharp increase in recent years. This category in turn can be disaggregated into two subsets: "interest earnings"[3] and "other miscellaneous revenues." In one study that analyzed this disaggregation (Swartz 1990), it was found that interest earnings accounted for approximately one-third of the increase in miscellaneous revenues from 1978 to 1987, while the "other" category was responsible for the remaining two-thirds. It is reasonable to assume that presently interest earnings are unlikely to exceed this one-third upper limit. Indeed if data were available, they would likely demonstrate that local governments currently receive little from interest earnings compared to what they earned in the 1980s. There are two contributing factors: First, interest rates have fallen dramatically. In the 1980s, the prime rate charged by banks averaged 11.8 percent. This has fallen to 10.0 percent in 1990, 8.46 percent in 1991, and all the way down to 6.0 percent in midsummer 1992. Second, and perhaps most important, after more than a decade of belt-tightening, there is simply little prospect of budget surpluses to magically reappear. Cities have postponed capital expenditure projects, cut service levels, frozen salaries, borrowed to the limit, and depleted their accumulation funds. In short, there still may be ways to generate savings, but the obvious, politically easy methods have long disappeared. This is reflected in the data. State and local budget surpluses throughout the 1980s averaged $40 billion annually. In 1990 and 1991 they averaged only $27.6 billion. Given the sluggish economy, there is no reason to believe that these surpluses will return to the 1980s levels.

This leaves us with the "other miscellaneous revenue" category. There is no official published definition for this category, but the computer record used by the staff of the Advisory Commission on Intergovernmental Relations (ACIR) lists the following items:[4] special assessments, sale of property (housing) and urban renewal, sale of property (other), fines and forfeits, rents and royalties, donations, net lottery revenue, and not elsewhere classified. These items are at least loosely related to user charges and certainly reflect the move toward privatizing and/or marketizing local government activities.

As Table 1.3 suggests, about 9 percent of the total revenue available to local governments comes from this vaguely specified revenue category (the difference between "charges/misc" and "charges only"). This is up from a mere 1.5 percent in 1978 and represents a sixfold increase in local government use of property sales, rents and royalties, fines, donations, and special measurements. (Note that lottery income falls into this category, but it is unlikely to be a source of revenue for local governments.) Whether local governments can expect these funds to be available throughout the 1990s is truly unclear.

Some Unfortunate Implications

The dramatic change in the U.S. system of fiscal federalism has gained widespread recognition in recent years. However, the full consequences of this redistribution in terms of fiscal responsibil-

ity are only now becoming obvious as urban finance comes under
siege in certain parts of the country.

What is clear is that our system of fiscal federalism has moved
away from making conscious attempts to "level-up" those governmental units that are most lacking in fiscal capacity. We are in
an era of fend-for-yourself federalism. In this new environment,
local governments must find sources of funds to support an ever-
expanding expenditure load. Some local governments will have
little difficulty meeting this challenge, but, as Table 1.3 suggests,
others must struggle.

Unfortunately, the states and local governments that are most
negatively impacted are often governmental units least capable of
handling this increased fiscal responsibility. A disproportionate
number of the "losers" in Table 1.3 are states with low fiscal
capacity. Indeed, with the exception of New York and Hawaii,
the other eight states have average per capita incomes below the
national average. In some cases, such as Mississippi, Louisiana,
and Oklahoma, per capita income is substantially below the national average. Only time will tell whether or not the fend-for-
yourself federalism will turn the clock back on the economic
development of these areas and create some kind of second-class
citizenship for those who are trapped in cities that are in a downward economic spiral.

Of related concern is how these adversely impacted cities have
responded to the shortfall in intergovernmental revenues. A worrisome pattern emerges. There is a renewed dependence on property
taxes and local governments have turned to a broad array of stopgap
sources of revenue: special assessments, sale of property, fines and
forfeits, rents, donations, and interest earnings. These sources of
revenue have serious limitations both in terms of their future revenue potential and in terms of their distributional consequences.

The Property Tax Base

One immediate concern for those responsible for ensuring the
adequacy of revenues to support the growing fiscal obligations of

local government is the stability of the property tax base. Erosion of this base at the very time that we anticipate that a greater dependency will be placed on the property tax could prove to be disastrous. As Dick Netzer points out in chapter 3, the property tax base has endured a systematic narrowing in the post–World War II period. The question that is raised in the Follain and Reschovsky chapters is whether or not there is a new threat to this critically important tax base.

Residential Property Markets

The initial concern that the residential component of the property tax base was deteriorating at an alarming rate was raised in 1989 by Gregory N. Mankiw and David N. Weil (see also Laing 1989), who argued that the real estate industry was in the midst of a catharsis. Housing values were falling in many communities, and in some communities they were falling precipitously. Mankiw and Weil based their projections on the abrupt change in our national demographies. For nearly forty-five years we had been the beneficiaries of a booming housing market. The boom began in the immediate postwar years as the returning veterans placed an extraordinary burden on the construction industry. These vets wanted single-dwelling houses, and they wanted them constructed quickly Thus, the demand for housing increased, and, as a result, the price of housing began a forty-year upward spiral. As the national economy successfully converted from a wartime economy to a peacetime economy and the numbers of the middle class swelled to record levels, the demand for new housing units continued at record levels through the 1950s and well into the 1960s. At that point in our history a new force was introduced into the housing marketplace: the "baby boomers" came of age. Like their parents, they demanded single-dwelling housing units, and they had the dollars to back up their demand.

However, the baby boom of the 1940s and 1950s was replaced by the baby bust of the 1960s and 1970s. Mankiw and Weil and others argue that this decline in birth rates is a major contributing factor to the weakness in many regional housing markets. Since the babies born in 1963 are the thirty-year-old demanders of housing in 1993, the potential consequence of the baby bust is immediate and apparently obvious. We have fewer new demanders in the marketplace. As we look backward along the successively younger age cohorts, we find the ranks thin. The relatively few that were born in the 1960s and 1970s will create only 1.1 million new households in the 1990s. This is a clear departure from our recent experience when the creation of 1.7 million households a year was not uncommon.

When these demographics are coupled with the economic parameters found in Table 1.4, there is serious cause for concern. Not only is there a dwindling number of potential home buyers, but during the 1980s, and into the foreseeable future, real per capita income was low by historic standards, while real mortgage interest rates were high. That is to say, the two most important determinants of housing demand, besides the number of buyers in the marketplace, are moving in the wrong direction to stimulate a reversal in either the growth rate in the housing stock or the rate of change in housing prices.

This meager growth rate of 1.2 percent in the per capita U.S. housing stock has a direct impact on the property tax base. In the 1960s and the 1970s, local governments could count on a growth rate twice as high. These additions to the tax base in part could finance new local government expenditures. Perversely, just as local governments were expected to assume a greater expenditure load, the growth of the residential portion of their property tax base begins to slow.

This is not offset by vigorous growth in the value of the existing housing stock. In real terms, the rate of change in housing prices was negative for the 1980–90 period. That is, once the nominal change of +3.6 percent is adjusted downward by the GDP price deflator of 5.1 percent, prices fell on the average of –2.9 percent. In the 1970s, the real change was +2.2 percent (+9.2 percent less the deflator of 7.0 percent), and in the 1960s, the real change in the value of the housing stock re-

Table 1.4

Economic Factors Affecting the Growth Rate in Housing Stock per Capita

	1980–90 (in percent)	1970–79 (in percent)	1960–69 (in percent)
Growth Rate of Housing Stock per Capita	1.2	2.4	2.3
Rate of Change in Housing Prices	3.6	9.2	2.5
Growth Rate in Real Income per Capita	1.5	2.3	2.8
Real Mortgage Rate*	6.5	1.8	3.5

Source: Keith M. Carlson, "Why Did Housing Growth Slow in the 1980s?" *National Economic Trends* (St. Louis: Federal Reserve Bank of St. Louis, April 1992).
*The difference between the new home mortgage rate and the inflation rate as measured by the GDP deflator.

mained about constant at –0.2 percent (+2.5 percent less a deflator of –2.7 percent).

Consequently, the growth in the property tax base in the 1980s and thus far in the 1990s that is attributable either to new home construction or to increases in the price of the existing housing stock is not keeping pace with the rate of inflation. Thus, to simply stand still and provide a constant level of real spending local governments have to increase their tax rates. Obviously, with the shifting pattern of fiscal federalism, which offloads obligations from the federal government and the state governments to local governments, there is increasing pressure on these lower levels of government to raise their property tax rates.

Commercial Property Markets

Much to the misfortune of local government officials, the story does not end here. At the same time that there is considerable weakness in the residential component of the property tax base, there has been a near collapse in the value of the commercial

portion of the property tax base. Commercial property accounts for 15 percent of the total property tax base and a substantially higher proportion of the urban property tax base. The
weakness found there may be even more long lasting than in
the residential markets.

The boom-bust cycle began in the early months of the
Reagan administration. The Economic Recovery Tax Act of
1981 not only cut the personal income taxes of high-income
Americans, suddenly leaving them with after-tax dollars to invest, but at the same time it provided generous tax advantages
to investments in commercial property. These changes in the
capital gains tax and in depreciation rules occurred just as the
"thrifts" were about to be given license to speculate in commercial property and foreigners were induced by tax breaks to
invest in the United States. The combined effect set in motion
an explosion of investment in commercial property. New long-
term loans for commercial property development rose from
$20 billion in 1981—an annual investment much in line with
the 1970s experience—to $150 billion in 1986. (Total mort-
gage indebtedness for commercial property rose from $255.5
billion in 1980 to $555 billion in 1986.)

The bust portion of the cycle can be traced to the 1986 Tax
Reform Act. Not only did this legislation rescind the special tax
advantages given to investment in property development, but in
addition it increased the marginal tax rates of high-income taxpayers by creating "passive income" as a class of income that
was now taxable. All rental income was placed in this new tax
class. Thus, investors in property development saw the present
value of their future earnings fall by at least 10 percent and in
some estimates by as much as 20 percent. In spite of these apparent adverse effects on property development investments, new
investment continued at historically high levels. New long-term
commercial lending did not peak until 1988, and the total outstanding debt edged upwards to $750 billion in 1989, when the
bubble finally burst.

The net result of all this was the construction of a massive over-supply of commercial floor space—offices, apartments, shops, and warehouse space. The 12.5 billion square feet of commercial space created in the 1980s was by most estimates 10 to 20 percent more than we needed. Commercial prices fell sharply, leaving few if any significant markets unaffected and devastating some markets where the speculation raged on well beyond reason.

Unfortunately, a sagging economy that is experiencing an extremely weak recovery and may slip back into recession is hardly vibrant enough to work off this over-supply. Consequently, not only will less new construction be added to the property tax base of urban America in the immediate future, but the value of existing property is unlikely to appreciate anywhere near the current rate of inflation, even though this inflation rate is at a twenty-year low. Of course, as in the case of residential property, the Federal Reserve System's attempt to produce a zero rate of inflation by keeping real interest rates, particularly the long end of the rate structure, at high levels will not hasten the recovery of this overextended market.

The Cost to Cities

At best, property values—both residential and commercial—and the property tax base that is dependent upon those values, will flatten out and perhaps rise marginally. At worst, property values in real terms—adjusted for inflation—could decline throughout the 1990s. But please note, even a moderate increase in these values will not be sufficient to offset the fiscal consequences of devolution that our local governments continue to experience. It would appear that the only way that local governments can survive in this post-Reagan world of decentralized government is by increasing the rates of the dreaded property tax. This has historically proven to be politically unpopular in nearly every taxing jurisdiction where it has been tried, and in some communities it has proven to be an "end-game" strategy as mobile, more affluent taxpayers flee the higher tax area in search of lower tax havens.

The Besieged City

In light of the bleak prospects for many of our cities in the remaining years of the twentieth century, some of the nation's most prominent economists were invited to address the issues raised in this introductory chapter: Are the problems of the "city" overstated? Is the property tax up to the task of supporting a new, expanded fiscal role for local governments? Do we need to be concerned with the flagging real estate markets? Are the revenue systems of local governments sufficiently diversified to spread the new fiscal federalism burden beyond the broad shoulders of the property tax? What can state governments do to lessen the burdens of their fiscally stressed cities? And, can cities pull themselves up by the bootstraps when the national economy seems to have lost its confidence and its place in the world economy? These and many related questions are addressed in the pages that follow.

Our first essay is authored by Katharine Lyall, the president of the University of Wisconsin System and deputy assistant secretary for economic affairs at the U.S. Department of Housing and Urban Development during the Carter administration. In her chapter, entitled "The Nation's Cities: Is History About to Be Repeated?" she argues that the fiscal environment in which cities operate is fundamentally shaped and determined by national economic conditions and federal policies. She details the consequences of the shifting fiscal federalism of the Reagan and Bush administrations, which has resulted in the termination of many federal programs targeted for cities and has placed the expenditure responsibility for an increasing number of many basic government programs squarely on the shoulders of state and local governments regardless of their fiscal capacity to manage them. For Lyall, the new fiscal federalism highlights the structural nature of the problems confronted by cities, which will not disappear once the national economy regains its vitality. In brief, it is reminiscent of the benign neglect that characterized federal policies in the 1950s and early 1960s.

Given the need to generate new revenues to replace the grants-in-aid that have vanished in this age of devolution, we next turn to Dick Netzer, the leading authority on the most important source of local government tax revenue: the property tax. Netzer, who currently serves as professor of economics and public administration at New York University and senior fellow of the Urban Research Center, traces the importance of the property tax over time in his chapter, "Property Taxes: Their Past, Present, and Future Place in Government Finance." Netzer documents the systematic erosion of the property tax base that has occurred over the past four decades. This narrowing of the base limits the revenue productivity of this tax as local governments search for new sources of funds, while at the same time it imposes serious equity and efficiency consequences. Thus, Netzer does not see the property tax playing a larger role in local government finance in the near future.

Our next chapter, contributed by James R. Follain, professor of economics and chair of the Economics Department at Syracuse University, addresses the issue of whether or not the dire predictions of Mankiw and Weil are a real threat to the property tax base as we approach the twenty-first century. He concludes that Mankiw and Weil have overstated the case. Follain's "optimistic" assumptions for estimating the real value of the *aggregate* stock of owner-occupied housing forecasts a real increase by as much as 10 percent during the next decade. Even his "pessimistic" assumptions generate positive real increases in value as we enter the twenty-first century. He does admit, however, that his aggregate data, which adds together urban, suburban, and rural housing markets, hide the special problems of urban areas.

This naturally takes us to Andrew Reschovsky's essay, which examines on a case-by-case basis how declining property values—both residential and commercial—have impacted the property tax base. Reschovsky is well versed in this area. He currently is a professor of agricultural economics and public affairs at the University of Wisconsin at Madison and serves as a fiscal consultant for a number of state and local governments throughout the country. In his chapter, "Are City Fiscal Crises on the Horizon?" Reschovsky finds that some cities are insulated from the collapse in market values by their fractional property tax assessments. (Control legislation passed in the late 1970s and early 1980s in some cases limited the amount of increased property value that could be captured by the assessed value. Since increased values in the boom period are not in the assessment base, decreased values in the bust portion of the cycle are also excluded from the base.) However, cities in other states that are not insulated in this fashion are negatively impacted immediately and significantly. Reschovsky concludes that an examination of the overall fiscal capacity of our nation's cities makes it difficult to be optimistic regarding the long-run fiscal health of our large metropolitan areas.

Chapter six looks to the future. It is authored by social critic William K. Tabb, who is a professor of economics and sociology at Queens College. Tabb's essay, "What Are the Limits of Government? What Are Its Obligations?" begins by examining the shift in "mainstream urbanist thinking" from redistributive liberalism to neo-conservatism. He describes the changing role of the federal government and analyzes the fiscal problems that this has caused our urban communities. Tabb argues that current trends in public policy must be reversed if we are to achieve social efficiency. Indeed, redesigning urban policy is a necessary precondition if we are serious in our attempts to restore our international competitiveness.

In the final chapter of this book, my colleague Professor Frank Bonello looks with some longing at his boyhood days spent in inner city Detroit. The working-class neighborhood that shaped his life was systematically undermined and eventually destroyed by a series of public policies that were indifferent to the fate of those living there. He asks if this is the eventual fate of all middle class urban residents who currently live in our cities.

Thus, the purpose of this book is to examine how local governments are paying for our new system of fiscal federalism, which demands that they share an increasingly larger fiscal responsibility as we approach the twenty-first century. Some local governments will thrive in this new environment. They will become the "winners"—if they are not already the winners—in this competitive federalism that we have put in place. What is uncertain is the future of the losers. Will these local communities find the resources to fund basic government services? Will we see large numbers of communities stagnate and perhaps even die? Will we as a society be willing to accept the human toll that is implicit in pitting community against community, state against state, and region against region in the hope of reaping the economic benefits of competition? Only time will tell, but there is not great optimism in many of the essays that follow.

Notes

1. State and local governmental data are often not disaggregated, since, as in the case of a federal grant for education, the grant must pass through state government but ultimately will be spent at the local level.
2. The phrase comes from John Shannon, "Federal and State-Local Spenders Go Their Separate Ways," in Robert J. Dilger, editor, *American Intergovernmental Relations Today,* New York: Prentice Hall, 1986.
3. The U.S. Department of Commerce defines interest earnings as interest earned on deposits and securities, including amounts for accrued interest on investment securities sold. However, receipts for accrued interest on bonds issued are classified as offsets to interest expenditure. Interest earnings do not include earnings on assets of employee-retirement systems.
4. This listing was obtained from Mr. Clay Dursthoff of the ACIR in a telephone conversation on January 26, 1990.

References

Laing, Jonathan R. 1989. "Crumbling Castles: The Recession in Real Estate Has Ominous Implications." *Barron's,* December 18.
Mankiw, Gregory N., and Weil, David N. 1989. "The Baby Boom, the Baby Bust, and the Housing Market," *Regional Science and Urban Economics,* May.
Shannon, John 1990. "The Deregulation of the American Federal System: 1789–1989," in *The Changing Face of Fiscal Federalism,* edited by

Thomas R. Swartz and John E. Peck (New York: M.E. Sharpe, Inc.).

Swartz, T.R, 1990. "The Cost of the New System of Fiscal Federalism in the U.S.," International Symposium on Fiscal Federalism, Seefeld/Tyrol, Austria: Institut für Finanzwissenschaft der Universersitat Innsbruck, March 16–17.

Tiebout, Charles M. "A Pure Theory of Local Expenditures," October 1956 *Journal of Political Economy,* pp. 416–24.

2

The Nation's Cities: Is History About to Be Repeated?

KATHARINE C. LYALL

This chapter considers the past and speculates about the future of American cities. What has happened to our cities since the 1960s? Can they survive into the next millennium in their current form? If not, what will our urban areas look like in the year 2000 and beyond? What will happen to the people who live and work in cities?

In thinking about these questions, we must recognize and consider the various, and changing, functions of cities. American cities are:

- economic machines
- political entities
- human service centers
- intellectual and creative centers
- international links to the global economy
- ports of entry and opportunity for immigrant populations

In short, our cities are complex entities serving complex social and economic functions; they are open to change from every side, most of it unplanned and unwanted. National trends and national policies determine the environment in which cities must operate and to which they must adapt.

National Urban Policy and Trends

The United States has not had an urban policy since the seventies, and it shows. Worse than benign neglect, the fiscal federalism of the eighties and nineties has meant the close-out of many federal programs targeted to cities and the simultaneous passing of responsibility for human services and economic development to state and local governments. Among the responsibilities handed over to states and localities are: K–12 educational reform, welfare assistance, low-income housing and care of the homeless, drug control, corrections, and environmental mandates. To these, state legislatures have added their own unfunded mandates for job assistance and training programs, health care for the indigent and uninsured, sewer and environmental projects, and local tax investment and enterprise zones.

In the decade of the 1980s, major federal programs targeted to cities were reduced by nearly half:

Table 2.1

**The Percentage Loss of Federal Programmatic
Grants to Cities,1980–91**

	1980–91 (in percent)
General revenue sharing	−95.9
Local public works	−56.7
Job training/service	−49.2
City water and sewer grants	−46.5
Energy conservation programs	−45.1
Community development block grants	−23.1
Mass transit	−48.0

Source: U.S. Office of Management and Budget, as reprinted in *Wisconsin State Journal,* February 4, 1992.

Table 2.2

The Percentage Growth of Federal Programs Directed toward Specific Populations

	1980–91 (in percent)
Interest expense	+248
Medicare	+222
Social Security	+130
Defense	+126

Source: U.S. Office of Management and Budget, as reprinted in *Wisconsin State Journal*, February 4, 1992.

At the same time, there was major growth in federal programs directed to a specific population segment—the elderly—and in federal obligations for interest on the debt and for defense. In short, the focus of federal policy and funding shifted from *places* to a specific segment of *people* comprising less than 20 percent of the population.

The president's proposed budget for FY 93 continues these patterns as shown in Figure 2.1. The graph shows clearly that the past thirty years have generated a more than fourfold increase in mandatory federal expenditures including deposit insurance (S&L bailout), federal retirement, means-tested entitlements, Medicaid, Medicare, Social Security, and Unemployment Insurance, while domestic discretionary spending—the category from which targeted assistance for cities must come—has risen about one-quarter as much over the same period. Thus, while mandatory expenditures were about 1.5 times domestic discretionary funding in 1962, in 1992 they are 3.94 times discretionary spending and growing.

Moreover, these trends are projected to continue unabated through 1997, based on the Bush administration's rather optimistic assumption of 3 percent average real annual growth in Gross Domestic Product through 1997 and continued low government borrowing rates. Because interest on federal debt now consumes one of every five federal revenue dollars, an increase in market interest rates can boost mandatory spending substantially. Thus, barring new federal tax increases, Figure 2.1 would appear to present a best-case scenario for the rest of the nineties.

Figure 2.1. **Trends in Mandatory vs. Discretionary Spending (1962–1997)***

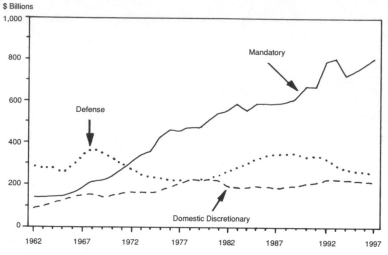

Notes: * Outlays in 1993 dollars.
Includes deposit and pension guarantees on a cash basis; excludes undistributed offsetting receipts.
Source: *Budget of the U.S. Government Fiscal Year 1993*, Part One—15 as reprinted in Council on Competitiveness, *A Competitiveness Assessment of the President's FY 1993 Budget*, Chart 1. (March 1992)

Underlying this fend-for-yourself federalism for cities have been the dual pincers of property tax reduction and the "no new taxes" pledge taken by federal, state, and local legislators alike. Not surprisingly under these conditions, the continued demand for government services was met through a ballooning in federal borrowing that was mirrored in local borrowing. The erosion of cities' most important single revenue source, the property tax, without authorization to tap replacement sources, and the escalation of service needs and mandates combined to leave no alternative to expanded borrowing.

The Past: How We Got Here

Although concern for cities first emerged in the public health, housing, and social welfare policies of the 1930s, both the level and the focus of urban concerns have changed with the larger economic environment of the nation. Through World War II, American cities housed the majority of the American population, industrial and commercial activity, and cultural life. City life provided the counterpoint to agriculture and attracted flows of population seeking career opportunities and a diverse dynamic society unavailable in rural life. Transportation and communications links focused attention on city centers as hubs of economic, political, and social activity. While cities grew at the periphery with the extension of trolley and bus lines, this growth was slow, and attention still focused inward on the city center.

The decades of the fifties and sixties produced dramatic changes. Federal policy supported construction of the nation's first interstate highway system, which gave strong impetus to industrial and communal development and forged a single large national market that became the engine of enormous economic expansion. At the same time, a new federal mortgage program for the first time brought homeownership within the grasp of moderate-income, blue-collar households. Together, working in symbiosis, the new federal highway and housing programs created perfect conditions for explosive suburban development. New housing, instead of growing in in-fill spaces within existing urban boundaries (and adding to the urban tax base) leaped those boundaries and escaped the urban tax base. Serving at first as bedroom communities from which workers still commuted to work and shop in the city, by the sixties many suburbs had also attracted retail and commercial activities from city centers. Shopping malls and professional offices sprouted in new, lower-cost suburban facilities, and retail activity in many city centers began to die out. New housing activity also declined within cities, and traditional neighborhoods began to transform, change character, and "filter" to lower-income population segments. Racial change was an important part of this process, made more tense by the growing sensitivity to civil rights in the nation at large. For the most part, however, cities maintained their manufacturing job base through the fifties and sixties and drew their workforce from

nation or decline in the Midwest; the latter half of the eighties has almost reversed those patterns, with stagnation or decline in the Northeast, South, and Midwest and a resurgence of growth in the West and mid-Atlantic regions. We must note, however, that the economic fate of central cities has been remarkably the same, regardless of their region.

Other characteristics of the deindustrialization of our metro areas have been: (1) a sharp decline in good-paying, entry-level jobs for those with low educational attainment—education at least through high school has become an essential pass to economic opportunity and self-support in our society, and those who, for whatever reason, do not attain this education threshold face increasingly bleak prospects—(2) a disproportionate number of undereducated citizens in the cities, a dilemma compounded by race. Among the Big Ten central cities in 1980 less than one-third of all jobs were held by people without a high school degree. In Baltimore, for example, approximately 30 percent of those employed in 1980 had less than a high school education; for the city's African-American residents, this figure was 50.6 percent. By 1990, these figures are undoubtedly much lower.

What this tells us is that many of the citizens of our central cities are less and less qualified to follow the employment base that is moving to the suburbs—even if the compounding problems of transportation and racism were to vanish. In short, the people-base and the economic-base of our cities are increasingly mismatched.

In America's Big Ten cities, the probability of getting a job is significantly increased by completion of high school and boosted further by graduation from college. For example, in Baltimore an African-American high school dropout has only a 56 percent probability of being employed; if he finishes high school, the probability of employment jumps to 74 percent; if he finishes college, the probability rises to 83 percent. The parallel probabilities for whites are about 10 percentage points higher at each education level (Kasarda 1990, Tables 8A, 11A).

City governments, local school districts, parent-teacher associations, and business-school partnerships are all working frantically to raise high school graduation rates and to improve the quality of what is learned in school. It is a race with time that has exceedingly high stakes, for a lost generation of youth represents not only great personal tragedy but a significant decline in the American labor force as it faces increasing international competition. It is for this latter reason that the problem of educational underattainment must be seen not only as a local but also as a national priority; not only a public need but a private one as well.

What does all this economic restructuring actually mean for inner-city neighborhoods? How have they been affected by these trends that wash over the larger region?

To understand what this has meant, I ask you to recall that in our older industrial cities, neighborhoods usually originated around a particular employer or industrial plant. Workers established residences within walking or streetcar distance from the plant, and frequently the personal and social relationships forged at work translated directly into neighborhood solidarity. Some, not all, employers recognized their interdependence with the neighborhood and consciously contributed to civic improvement projects. Vestiges of this orientation around a particular kind of employment lingered well into the seventies, defining the characteristics of neighborhoods and the way residents thought of themselves—it gave neighborhoods distinct identities.

The economic restructuring of the seventies and eighties erased the final traces of this identity and supplied no alternative organizing principle in its place. Aside from a short dalliance with "gentrification" of some neighborhoods in the seventies and eighties, market forces have created incentives that press inexorably for *escape* from the old neighborhoods, not for renovation or renewal. The final blows were struck in the eighties by the dramatic reduction of federal support for housing and community development efforts. The doctrine of fiscal federalism shifted responsibility—largely without resources—to states and cities, where housing and neighborhood revitalization have to compete with a host of other claims on the local resource base.

A number of observers, including William Julius Wilson at the University of Chicago and Isabelle Sawhill of the Urban Institute, believe that these trends, working their way through the economy, have created an urban "underclass" that is increasingly isolated in the inner cities (Wilson 1987; Sawhill 1975). Wilson notes that those blacks that have succeeded in raising educational and economic attainment, like their white counterparts, have moved out, following the employment base and the good life, leaving behind those without models of personal success. One observer has noted that whereas neighborhoods used to be defined by their employment base, many are now defined by their drug-trading territories, and choice of neighborhood can protect a family from or expose it to the drug culture.

Some sociologists are now asking: Are neighborhoods part of the problem or part of the solution? Are they traps for the underclass or buffers that can provide social support and opportunities for minority entrepreneurship? Do poor neighborhoods have "contagion effects" on behavior—through the drug culture and lack of successful role models—or can they be enlisted to fight these elements?

To summarize, central city neighborhoods have experienced:

• economic restructuring away from manufacturing and good-paying entry-level jobs and an economic migration of employment and people to the suburbs;

• a shift of employment opportunities to services, many requiring higher educational attainment;

• a dramatic slowing of housing renovation and reconstruction opportunities;

• the rise of an underclass increasingly isolated from jobs, social services, and opportunities;

• the rise of the drug culture in many neighborhoods;

• the declining importance of employers as the organizing focus for neighborhoods.

Thus, for many urban neighborhoods, as Gertrude Stein said, "There's no there there."

Marshall Kaplan (1990, 293–302) suggests that past neighborhood policies have had mixed results because they have been
guided by no clear or consistent theory that links metropolitan
growth to neighborhood change. In the past, neighborhood initiatives have often been too ambitious ("un-doable") so that
they were set up for failure from the beginning. The real but
modest gains actually achieved were overshadowed by a visible failure to meet the unrealistically high goals touted for
such efforts.

Another and more important problem is our pursuit—at both
the federal and the local levels—of two sets of strategies that
have been mutually offsetting. We have used people-oriented
approaches, such as the War on Poverty, which defined neighborhood problems as poverty problems and were structured to help
people escape their neighborhoods. At the same time, we have
used place-oriented strategies, such as Model Cities, to help people
stay in their neighborhoods. With no coordination or linkage, many
of our "place policies" work counter to our "people policies."

The confusion of goals and the apparent failure of these
programs to rebuild neighborhoods led conservatives in the
eighties to declare that these should not be legitimate national
concerns at all.

Thus, as noted earlier, the federal urban policy of the eighties
has been marked by withdrawal, denial, and massive disinvest-
ment. Federal housing assistance programs—for construction,
renovation, and rental assistance—have been eliminated or cut
by as much as 80 percent. Urban Development Action Grants
(UDAG) and Community Development Block Grants (CDBG),
which had provided the seed money and the federal
government's matching contribution to local and private sector
investments in community development, were drastically cut or
eliminated on the grounds that the nation could no longer afford
to participate in a "strictly local" problem. Fiscal federalism, and
a mounting federal deficit, shifted down to cities and municipali-
ties full responsibility for housing, urban infrastructure, education, and most social services except Social Security and

Medicare. Even the responsibility for fighting the war on drugs—surely a problem that transcends local jurisdictional boundaries if ever there was one—was laid primarily at the door of states and local governments.

States and localities have done their best to address these problems, even increasing taxes when necessary to do so. As the crisis deepens, it has also stimulated an increase in private support for some of these needs through business and school initiatives, special housing partnerships, and a variety of quasi-public and public-private ventures. Some cities have become very creative in developing such partnerships; others, such as Detroit, Philadelphia, and New York, appear to be sinking under the weight of accumulated burdens that swamp *all* available resources, public and private.

The Future: Where Are We Going?

If the forties and fifties produced mainly "in-fill" growth of cities within their borders and the sixties and seventies saw the development of full-blown, free-standing suburbs, the eighties and nineties are marked by selected rural development and the growth of what Joel Garreau has called "edge cities" at the periphery of major urban areas. In *U.S. News and World Report,* he described edge cities this way:

> An edge city is a 21st-century information-age, middle-class place that almost never matches political boundaries on a map. It has at least as much office space as Memphis and contains at least one medium-sized mall with world-class department stores and up to 100 shops. It has more jobs than bedrooms. This is not a suburb; it is its own urb. People head toward it, not away from it, when the day begins.

Garreau estimates that there are some two hundred edge cities in the United States, including places like Tysons Corner, Virginia; Irvine, California; and Las Colinas, near Dallas, Texas.

Established at the intersection of freeways, these edge cities offer ready auto and truck access to workers and to shippers of goods. Edge cities provide a safe, convenient workplace, attractive to a suburban workforce composed increasingly of women. This movement of jobs has been aided by the freedom that information technology provides for companies to spin off whole functions to remote locations. But it also has a dark side: the geographic and psychological separation of jobs and middle-class population from the cities they surround. And, as Herbert J. Gans points out, these are jobs, retail sales, and office spaces not located in or contributing to the tax base of cities.

A continued decline in Americans' real standard of living will continue to draw women into the workforce and move them from part-time to full-time positions in the labor force. This places a premium on convenient, safe, accessible workplaces, shopping, and child care. Continued suburban and edge-city growth seems likely, and with it a waning sense of shared fate or responsibility for cities. Without a conscious national urban policy, the political influence of cities seems destined to wane through the nineties.

The Fiscal Condition of Cities

The stories of such East Coast and Midwest cities as Boston, Milwaukee, New York, and Philadelphia trace out the enormous shifts and pressures to which cities have been subjected in the eighties. While the needs of an increasingly dependent urban population have grown, the greatest changes have occurred in the shifting revenue sources available to cities, as well as certain limitations imposed by state referenda and mandates. Proposition 2½, for example, has removed an estimated $78 million from Boston's annual tax revenues, over and beyond reductions in the property tax base occasioned by falling property values. At the same time, growth of state aid and shared revenues declined, as states themselves retained more revenues to meet federal mandates and to solve their own deficits.

The U.S. Census Bureau's *State Government Finances* shows that state aid to local governments, which was increasing at 10–15 percent a year in the early eighties, by the end of the decade was rising at less than half that rate (Gold & Ritchie 7n). This is notable in light of the fact that many states have automatic revenue-sharing increases built into their local aid formulas. In 1991, for example, Illinois revised its income tax revenue-sharing formula to reduce local receipts by half, Rhode Island reduced its reimbursement for local hospital services by 20 percent and North Carolina froze aid to local governments and reduced the shared fraction of shared state-local revenues. Local governments have raised fines, fees, and user charges, most notably fees for public hospital services; drained special funds and reserves; turned to lottery receipts to support essential services; and accelerated the timing of tax receipts to meet payrolls and debt payments.

Some cities, such as Philadelphia, clutched by protracted political paralysis, have been virtually cut off from the capital market by below-investment-grade credit ratings, which make their bonds ineligible for purchase by pension funds and other large institutional investors.

The notable feature of city fiscal distress in the nineties is that deficits are *structural,* not temporary, and require structural, not temporary, solutions. Structural problems include the facts that:

• in many states, progressive property and income taxes are constitutionally prohibited, thus denying state and local governments the benefits of growth in tax bases;

• many cities located within large counties must provide and pay for, but cannot control, county-mandated service costs;

• many urban areas need regional solutions to the problems of mass transit, waste management, and communication;

• virtually all cities (and not a few states) need to commit to training and development of their employees for modern, client-oriented service delivery and the adoption of such established techniques as automated property appraisal systems, procurement reforms, timely payment of vendors, professional pension fund management, and solvency.

The political fallout of fiscal federalism has been as significant for states and localities as the financial effects. To the chagrin of many conservatives, instead of getting government off the backs of taxpayers, the federalism of the eighties has produced huge growth in state government. During the eighties, state spending doubled, from $258 billion to $525 billion, and the number of state employees grew concomitantly—big government simply moved closer to the taxpayer.

As Virginia I. Postrel (1991) notes:

> On the regulatory level, state activism works in one direction: toward bigger government and more restrictive regulations. States aren't allowed to pass low minimum wages, weaker environmental controls or simpler labeling laws than the federal government. But, unless otherwise specified, they can always pass more stringent laws.

Moreover, a decade of responsibilities passed down from the federal to state and state to local governments has toughened the independent attitudes and outlook of many city officials. As Jonathan Walters (1992) puts it: "City officials are taking one simple message to state legislators in 1992: If states can't do much to solve city problems ... then get out of the way and give local governments the tools to do the job themselves." And Edward Farrell worries that: "State governments and Washington have stopped looking at us [cities] as the providers of basic public services, and have started viewing local governments as another interest group."

To compensate, some states have recently begun to enhance local ability to raise revenue by granting local governments authority to levy income taxes or to increase the maximum sales tax levy. Others have begun to sort out and take over certain functions formerly the responsibility of local government. Most commonly, *states* are moving to take over responsibility for the courts, prisons, jails, and the cost of public defenders offices, while *localities and counties* are taking specific responsibility for mental health, indigent care, the administrative cost of Medicaid audits, and general assistance.

In general, states seem to be reducing specific aid transfers in exchange for sharing new revenue sources with their local governments and streamlining many smaller programs into one. In turn, changes being made in the eligibility rules for AFDC and general assistance may throw increased caseloads onto county programs that take up the slack.

Thus, we see the first imperfect gropings toward a restructuring of local revenues and functional responsibilities. It appears that most states understand the plight of their cities and want to respond within the constraints imposed by their own fiscal condition. A notable exception is the area of unfunded state mandates, where, despite growing complaints, states and the courts continue to require expansion of local services for everything from juvenile detention services to solid-waste recycling and retirement payments. Some of these mandates undoubtedly reflect the disjointed nature of state policymaking, which obscures the interactive effects of complex social services decisions across a wide variety of local, county, and state constituencies.

Conclusion: What the Crystal Ball Shows

So we come finally to the intriguing question posed in the title to this paper: *Is history about to repeat itself for our cities?* Having struggled to renew themselves physically and financially throughout the past two decades, are U.S. cities caught once again in a downward spiral of fiscal, social, and physical decay as they were in the sixties?

My crystal ball says the answer to this is Yes, but. . . . Cities are going to continue to wrestle the demons of poverty and physical and fiscal decay, *but* the division of responsibilities among levels of government and the resource bases from which these problems are addressed will change dramatically in this decade. Moreover, the political clout of both cities and the Congress will wane, while that of the states grows.

The political clout of most large cities, especially those in the Northeast and Midwest, will decline, reflecting population shifts and reapportionments documented in the 1990 census. Some southern and many western cities will continue to grow, primarily reflecting growing minority populations. Congress, on the other hand, will find itself increasingly "marginalized" by the overhanging federal deficit and the growth of entitlements for the elderly, which leave few opportunities for new programs or federal interventions in state and local concerns. In short, the future of American cities will lie increasingly with themselves and the state governments that created them. The centrifugal forces of fiscal federalism set in motion in 1980 will continue to the end of the decade before a correction occurs.

The crystal ball also reveals:

• *Continued fiscal pressures*

Cities will have to pare down services and increase the efficiency of their delivery systems. No longer able to serve as employers of last resort for the unskilled, cities will look hard at unit costs and workers' training. Municipal workforces will increasingly be in competition with private providers of everything from garbage collection to education and "outsourcing" will become increasingly common.

Cities will strive to forge regional service agreements in which shared costs with other jurisdictions and even with private entities are advantageous. Moreover, the perception of acknowledged regional problems will expand to encompass not only traffic, land use, and pollution but welfare, homelessness, and K–12 education as well. City governments will be driven to adopt more sophisticated budgeting, forecasting, and management techniques that take account not only of state and local conditions but of national and international conditions as well. America's major cities will see themselves as part of the competitive global economy with American job opportunities and immigration determined by forces well beyond local control.

And local governments will succeed in pressing for the right to tap new revenue sources and in passing restrictions on unfunded state mandates.

• *Waning political influence*

All cities in the Northeast and Midwest are rapidly losing clout as a group to their suburbs and to the growing metropolitan areas of the West and Southwest. In 1992, only one-quarter of those eligible to vote will live in central cities—"A majority of votes will be cast in the suburbs." As *U.S. News and World Report* (December 30, 1991/January 6, 1992) notes: "1992's typical voter is ... a clerical worker in a suburban office tower who shops in a nearby mall and whose house is in a suburb several freeway exits away. She spends little or no time at work or at play in the central cities . . . ."

A single state, California, holds one-fifth of the nation's electoral votes required to win a presidential election, outweighing the voters of all other states west of the Mississippi!

This geographic partitioning of political power weakens a sense of economic reliance on central cities as well as a sense of responsibility for assisting those governments with services. As federal funds decline, the glue that made political coalitions between cities and their suburbs possible also weakens.

• *Growing cultural and workforce diversity*
Two out of every three new workforce entrants by the year 2000 will come from minority populations. Indeed, the 1990 census showed that California already has no single ethnic majority, with whites accounting for 49.8 percent of the population in 1990. Our urban populations are not only ethnically diverse but educationally diverse as well. It seems likely that the entrepreneurial and political leadership of our major cities will become significantly more diverse in the nineties. As this happens, we can expect to see increasing challenges to the use of race as a legitimate policy factor.

• *Infrastructure renewal*
Most older U.S. cities have fully depreciated infrastructure (roads, bridges, sewers) that cannot survive another decade; it must be refurbished or replaced before the nineties are out, or these cities will die as commercial and economic centers. (Death as a residential center takes a bit longer.) The good news is that construction is viewed as an appropriate jump-starter of economic activity in a recession, *and* state and local borrowing ca-

pacity is up, enabling public borrowing for such investment. The Public Securities Association reports that state and local governments borrowed $47 billion in 1991 for infrastructure, and that, as a whole, state and local governments have plenty of additional borrowing capacity for the future. Even states with debt limits can convert debt service to lease fees by using COPS (certificates of participation), through which a private leasing corporation retains ownership of the asset. The bad news may be that cities will have to pay dearly for these funds in competition with needs of the federal deficit and private industry.

In the end, cities must cope even if the federal government is no longer prepared to be a partner in these tasks. A new kind of public-private partnership is being developed in the nineties to cope with urban change. Neighborhoods are becoming tools for meeting the complex needs of urban populations in small-scale but innovative ways. Housing programs not only provide low-income housing opportunities, but are also becoming vehicles for job training,[1] local employment, and increased homeownership opportunities for moderate-income households. Neighborhood organizations are being refocused as effective partners in an integrated revitalization strategy, focusing *away* from the 1960s-style preoccupation with community control and "power processes" and *toward* a more pragmatic concern with resources and communication.

Langley Keyes (1990) has noted this more pragmatic approach emerging in recent years:

> In the current model [of neighborhood activism], professionals working for nonprofit organizations focus on specific deals which allocate public and private resources for services, jobs, housing, and economic development to the low income residents of the target area. The concepts of "deal making" and "entrepreneurship" seem more relevant to the activities of these local professionals than "participation" and "confrontation."

Repetition of riots in inner-city Los Angeles in the summer of

1992 once again raised questions about the need for a national urban policy. The driving focus of this renewed interest is on economics and race—on job opportunities and social justice. Congress, fearing a long, hot, rebellious summer in the cities during an election year, rushed through an emergency approval for $1 billion for inner-city jobs, but none of the presidential candidates talked of a national urban policy with much enthusiasm.

America is just beginning to wake up from its long sleep to recognize that its *people* are the key to its future in a competitive world, and that one-third of its people live in places that require some attention—our cities.

Notes

1. A series of demonstration programs, such as Ventures in Community Improvement (VICI), have been successfully conducted in a number of cities to train women in housing repair and renovation, for example. The results for programs in ten cities in which 385 women participated are reported in *Ventures in Community Improvement: Findings from a Four-Site Replication Initiative, 1984–87* (Philadelphia: Public/Private Ventures, Fall 1987).

References

Burtless, Gary. 1990. *A Future of Lousy Jobs?* Washington, D.C.: The Brookings Institution.
Danziger, Sheldon H., and Weinberg, Daniel H. 1986. *Fighting Poverty: What Works and What Doesn't*. Cambridge, Mass.: Harvard University Press.
Eisinger, Peter K., and Gormley, William. 1988. *The Midwest Response to the New Federalism*. Madison: University of Wisconsin Press.
Gans, Herbert J. 1991. "Life on the Edge of the City's Limits." *The Washington Post National Weekly,* September 9–15: 35.
Garreau, Joel. 1991a. "The Cities of the Future." *U.S. News and World Report,* September 23: 66–67.
———. 1991b. *Edge City: Life on the New Frontier*. New York: Doubleday.
Gold, Steven D., and Sarah Richie. 1991. *State Policies Affecting Cities and Counties in 1991: Shift and Shaft Federalism?* Nelson A. Rockefeller Institute of Government, State University at Albany, unpublished manuscript.
Gurwitt, Rob. 1992. "The Painful Truth about Cities and Suburbs: They Need Each Other." *Governing,* February: 56–60.

Haveman, Robert H. 1987. *Poverty Policy and Poverty Research*. Madison: University of Wisconsin Press.

Huey, John. 1991. "The Best Cities for Business." *Fortune*, November 4: 52–84.

Johnson, Brad C. 1991. "Washington Should Look at the Damage It's Doing." *The Washington Post National Weekly*, July 22–28: 23–24.

Kaplan, Marshall. 1990. "American Neighborhood Policies: Mixed Results and Uneven Evaluations." In Kaplan and James, eds., *The Future of National Urban Policy*, 293–302.

Kaplan, Marshall, and James, Franklin. 1990. *The Future of National Urban Policy*. Durham, N.C.: Duke University Press.

Kasarda, John D. 1990. "Jobs and the Underclass in Large and Mid-Size Metropolitan Areas." Unpublished paper.

Keyes, Langley. "The Shifting Focus of Neighborhood Groups: The Massachusetts Experience." In Kaplan and James, eds., *The Future of National Urban Policy*, 293–302.

Ladd, Helen F., and Yinger, John. 1989. *America's Ailing Cities*. Baltimore: Johns Hopkins Press.

Lemov, Penelope. 1992. "The Brave New World of Public Finance." *Governing*, February: 27–28.

Levy, Frank. 1987. *Dollars and Dreams: The Changing American Income Distribution*. New York: Russell Sage Foundation.

Mineta, Norman Y. "Time to Rebuild America." *State Government News*, November: 26–27.

Postrel, Virginia I. 1991. "States' Rights, or Dereliction of Duty?" *The Washington Post National Weekly*, July 22–28: 23.

Sawhill, I.; Peabody, G.E.; Jones, C.A.; and Caldwell, S.B. 1975. *Income Transfers and Family Structure*. Washington, D.C.: Urban Institute.

Schwartz, David C.; Ferianto, Richard C.; and Hoffman, Daniel N. 1988. *A New Housing Policy for America*. Philadelphia: Temple University Press.

Shalala, Donna E., and Vitullo-Martin, Julia. 1989. "Rethinking the Urban Crisis." *American Planning Association Journal*, Winter: 3–13.

Spiers, Joseph. 1991. "Scant Help from the States." *Fortune*, November 4: 21–24.

Walters, Jonathan. 1992. "Cities Have a Simple Message For States This Year: Set Us Free." *Governing*, January: 41–43.

Wilson, William Julius. 1987. *The Truly Disadvantaged: The Inner City, the Underclass and Public Policy*. Chicago: University of Chicago Press.

3

Property Taxes: Their Past, Present, and Future Place in Government Finance

DICK NETZER

The role of the property tax in local government finance has diminished drastically over the past sixty years. Just before the Great Depression of the 1930s, the property tax provided about two-thirds of all the revenue of American local governments, compared to about one-fourth today (see Table 3.1). However, that decline has not been continuous. The change in the role of the property tax occurred in two stages, the forties and the seventies, two episodes distinctly different from the long periods of stability in the relative role of the property tax that occurred before and after each of these two periods. Since roughly 1980, we have been in one of those periods of stability, possibly even in a period in which there may be a small reversal of the long decline. This is surprising because, simultaneously, the legal base of the property tax has continued to narrow, limitations on property tax rates and levies have spread, and abatements and exemptions for economic development purposes have spread even more. Thus, the absence of a decline in the property tax implies an increase in the burdens on that part of the nation's tangible wealth not excluded from the base or protected from the full rigors of the tax. But because every aspect of the property tax is highly varied geographically, the national statistics

Table 3.1

**The Property Tax and Local Government Revenue,
Selected Years 1902–89**

Property tax revenue as percent of —

	Personal income	Total local government revenue	All own-source revenue	Total tax revenue
1902	N.A.	68.3	72.7	88.6
1927	N.A.	68.8	76.1	97.3
1932	8.4	67.2	77.3	97.3
1940	5.4	54.0	72.0	92.7
1946	2.7	49.5	63.9	91.9
1950	3.1	43.7	60.3	88.2
1955	3.3	42.7	58.0	86.9
1960	3.9	42.3	58.0	87.4
1965	4.0	40.8	57.0	86.9
1966	4.0	40.2	57.6	87.4
1967	3.9	39.0	56.7	86.6
1968	3.8	38.2	56.1	86.1
1969	3.9	37.5	55.8	85.4
1970	4.0	37.0	55.3	84.9
1971	4.1	36.4	55.2	84.6
1972	4.3	36.2	55.3	83.7
1973	4.0	34.0	54.0	82.9
1974	3.9	32.4	52.4	82.2
1975	3.8	31.3	51.1	81.6
1976	3.8	30.8	50.5	81.2
1977	3.8	30.7	50.4	80.5
1978	3.5	29.9	49.1	79.7
1979	3.1	26.6	44.7	77.5
1980	2.9	25.4	42.1	75.9
1981	2.9	25.0	40.8	76.0
1982	3.0	25.0	39.7	76.1
1983	3.0	25.4	39.3	76.0
1984	3.0	25.3	38.7	75.0
1985	3.0	24.8	37.7	74.2
1986	3.1	24.7	37.3	74.0
1987	3.1	24.7	37.0	73.6
1988	3.1	25.7	38.3	74.1
1989	3.1	25.8	38.4	74.3

Source: U.S. Census Bureau, Government Finance diskettes, 1989.

hide considerable variation among and within regions, that is, from state to state.

The main goal of this chapter is to consider whether the property tax is likely to enter a new period of shrinkage in relative importance, or the reverse, and the implications of both trends—implications for the distribution of the tax burdens, the distribution of people and economic activity within and among regions, and the financing of public services. Also, do the likely trends suggest another period of tax revolts and new limitations? Before those prospective issues can be addressed, we need to consider the past and present, however.

The Past and Present Role of the Tax

The most important long-term effect of the Great Depression on American fiscal federalism was a profound and permanent change in the role of the federal government in American society, from an essentially peripheral financer of civilian public expenditure to its present central role. However, that took years to implement fully, and in the short run, the federal role in dollar terms remained modest in the 1930s and 1940s. What did change sharply in response to the collapse in property values and incomes and the severity of social problems during the Depression, was the role of the state governments. The first protracted decline in the role of the property tax shown in Table 3.1— during the 1930s and 1940s—was almost entirely a result of major increases in state government aid for important local government functions, notably education, welfare, health, and highways, financed by state government taxes on income, sales, and highway users.

In the first fifteen or so years after 1950, the relative role of the property tax changed little, as property values and effective property tax rates rose about as fast as local government expenditure. But the subsequent fifteen years—after 1965—witnessed another sharp decline. This decline was largely attributable to relatively increased state and federal aid to local governments, but in addi-

Figure 3.1. **Property Tax Revenue as Percent of Total State-Local Tax Revenue**

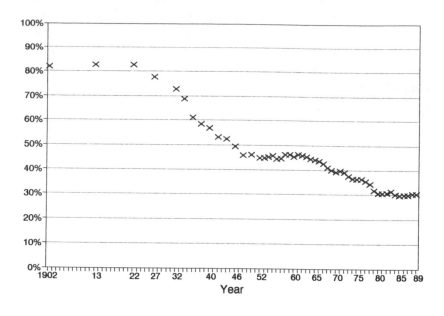

Source: U.S. Census Bureau

tion, the property tax lost ground to both local nonproperty taxes and, more significantly, to increased reliance on nontax revenues, especially user charges.

In the 1980s, as Table 3.1 shows, the property tax did not decline as a share of total local government revenue and declined very little relative to local nonproperty taxes, although the importance of user charges has continued to rise somewhat vis-à-vis the property tax.

In summary, the historic decline in the role of the property tax mostly reflects the decision, within the fifty state-local fiscal systems, to replace local property taxes with state (and, to a much lesser extent, local) nonproperty taxes, which is both a tax policy and a fiscal federalism decision. Figure 3.1 shows the declines and plateaus in property taxes as a percent of total state-local tax

Table 3.2

Role of the Property Tax in Local Government Revenue, By Type of Governmental Unit, 1979 and 1989

(Property tax revenue as percent of revenue aggregate shown)

	All general revenue	General revenue from own sources	Tax revenue
All local governments			
1978–79	29.5	53.3	77.5
1988–89	29.3	46.7	74.3
County governments			
1978–79	26.0	49.7	77.1
1988–89	27.9	43.7	72.9
Independent school districts			
1978–79	37.0	81.2	96.7
1988–89	36.2	79.3	97.5
53 largest cities			
1978–79	20.1	35.0	48.4
1988–89	19.9	28.9	42.5
45 largest cities without dependent schools			
1978–79	17.3	28.1	42.9
1988–89	18.7	24.0	40.9
Large cities with dependent schools: New York City			
1978–79	22.2	40.4	51.6
1988–89	20.2	32.1	41.3
7 other cities			
1978–79	23.2	45.1	55.9
1988–89	23.0	38.8	52.0
All smaller cities			
1978–79	25.6	39.9	63.5
1988–89	25.1	33.5	59.4

Source: U.S. Census Bureau, *Governmental Finances* and *City Government Finances* for 1978–79 and 1988–89.

collections. The other variables have been federal aid direct to local governments and nontax revenues. There was fairly steady relative growth in local nonproperty taxes until recently (see the last column of Table 3.1), but they continue to be only slightly more than one-fourth of local tax revenue.

So far, the discussion has dealt only with aggregates for all local governments. Table 3.2 identifies the role of the property tax in the finances of different types of units of local government over the last decade.[1] It is clear that the recent relative stability in the role of the property tax is largely attributable to school finance. The property tax role continued to shrink for county governments and for city governments, especially the larger cities. The municipal governments of the nation's larger cities now obtain more revenue from local nonproperty taxes than from the property tax, with the exception of a few that operate their own dependent school systems.

Regional Disparities

Table 3.3 indicates the geographic disparities in the role of the property tax as of 1989.[2] There are significant regional differences: the Northeast and Midwest rely more on the property tax than the South and West. But there are substantial intra-regional differences, including major disparities between adjacent states: Oregon and Washington, Mississippi and Alabama, New Jersey and Pennsylvania, Michigan and Ohio, Missouri and Kansas and Iowa, Virginia and North Carolina, Montana and Idaho, all combinations of states that do not differ enormously from one another *except* in regard to their tax systems. There are no obvious explanations for these differences between adjacent states in the choice among fiscal institutions.[3]

Changes in the Tax Base

In practice, the American property tax never was what it was supposed to be in law and in theory in the mid-nineteenth century: a general tax on the current value of all privately owned wealth. It was too easy to avoid entirely the taxation of some important types of assets and to undervalue drastically other types of assets. By the late nineteenth century, states had begun to narrow the reach of the tax to reduce the inequities associated with the resulting poor enforcement. In the early part of this century, further tax base narrowing was connected with the adoption of new forms of state taxation, which substituted for various components of the property tax in different states, including: the state corporate income tax for property taxes on business tangible personal property in Delaware, Pennsylvania, and New York; various state business taxes for property taxes on intangible personal property in the great majority of the states; state motor vehicle registration taxes for property taxes on motor vehicles in about half the states; state gross receipts taxes on utilities for property taxes on specific types of utilities in several states.

Economic adversity had strong effects on the coverage of the property tax. The agricultural depression of the 1920s led to the adoption of classification systems in Minnesota and Montana, providing for much reduced taxes on agricultural and homeowner residential property. This foreshadowed the more widespread adoption of restrictions in the 1930s, including large "homestead exemptions" in several states (in some cases, like Louisiana, coming close to excluding almost all owner-occupied nonfarm houses from the tax rolls), exemption of some or all agricultural personal property and household personal property in numerous states, and the adoption of property tax rate limits that truly were binding (rather than empty gestures) in a few states, notably Ohio and West Virginia. In the quarter century after 1940, the institutional structure of the property tax changed little, but during the past two decades the pace of structural change has been rapid.

Recent Tax Base Narrowing

One change has been the removal of ever more nonreal property, that is, property other than land and buildings, from the

Table 3.3

Regional and Intraregional Differences in the Role of the Property Tax in State–Local Tax Systems, 1989

(Property tax revenue as percent of total tax revenue of state and local governments combined)

U.S. mean	30.4
Northeast	32.1
New England	37.4
Connecticut	40.1
Massachusetts	32.3
Maine	34.1
New Hampshire	65.7
Rhode Island	38.7
Vermont	39.4
Middle Atlantic	32.3
New Jersey	43.4
New York	30.5
Pennsylvania	27.0
Midwest	33.0
East North Central	33.7
Illinois	35.2
Indiana	30.3
Michigan	38.4
Ohio	28.1
Wisconsin	35.2
West North Central	31.2
Iowa	35.5
Kansas	35.9
Minnesota	30.5
Missouri	21.8
North Dakota	29.9
Nebraska	41.5
South Dakota	41.1
South	27.4
South Atlantic	27.4
District of Columbia	31.7
Delaware	13.7
Florida	33.5
Georgia	27.2
Maryland	24.7
North Carolina	20.4
South Carolina	24.5
Virginia	29.4
West Virginia	17.9
East South Central	18.6
Alabama	11.9
Kentucky	16.4
Mississippi	24.6
Tennessee	22.6

Table 3.3 (continued)

West South Central	31.8
Arkansas	17.7
Louisiana	17.0
Oklahoma	18.1
Texas	39.2
West	27.9
Mountain	30.6
Arizona	32.6
Colorado	35.5
Idaho	27.6
Montana	43.6
New Mexico	11.6
Nevada	21.5
Utah	29.1
Wyoming	43.2
Pacific	27.2
Alaska	32.1
California	26.0
Hawaii	13.9
Oregon	44.0
Washington	28.4

Source: U.S. Census Bureau, Government Finance diskettes, 1989.

tax base, what is known as personal property in the law. Thirty years ago, virtually all personal property was exempt from tax in four states and motor vehicles in about half the states, but farm and nonfarm business inventories and equipment were taxable, with a few exceptions, in forty-six of the states. By 1989, personal property was entirely exempt in nine states; agricultural personal property was entirely exempt in ten other states and nearly exempt in several more; business inventories were generally taxable in fewer than ten states; and there were widespread exemptions of various types of business equipment, especially manufacturing machinery, in a good many states (*1987 Census of Governments;* Netzer 1966, chapter 6). State actions to exempt business personal property have been especially common in the late 1970s and 1980s.

Not surprisingly, the personal property share of the tax base declined from more than 17 percent of the tax base in 1956 to about 10 percent in 1986. This was in the face of a significantly more rapid increase in the market value of business equipment than of business structures during the same period (U.S. Department of Commerce 1987; Musgrave 1990). Had the property tax coverage of personal property remained unchanged, the personal property share of the property tax base would have increased, not declined.

In all but one of the states (Wisconsin),[4] the state governments have removed a substantial portion of the value of agricultural and other open-space land from the property tax rolls by providing that such land be taxed at its value in the current use, rather than at its market value. Except in wholly nonurban states, the actual economic value in the current uses often is far below the market value for alternative uses; in practice, farmland tends to be drastically underassessed even on a current-use basis, so that agricultural land is a very small component of the tax base even in Cornbelt states, for example, about one-eighth of total assessed value in Indiana. The formal provisions for preferential assessment of farmland almost all date from the mid-1960s. Consequently, property listed on the tax rolls as acreage and farms declined from about 10 percent of all assessment rolls in 1956 to about 6 percent in 1986 (Netzer 1966; *1987 Census of Governments*).

Until recently, nearly all states had formal requirements for uniformity of treatment of the property that is on the tax rolls (although systematic differences in assessment levels by type of property have been endemic), but by now fifteen states and the District of Columbia have what is known in the trade as "classification" systems, that is, formal provisions for dividing taxable property into use classes and either assessing the different classes at different percentages of market value or applying different tax rates to the assessed value of the property. Without exception, these systems tax owner-occupied residential property at the lowest effective rates; usually, farm property is equally favored (this is in addition to current-use valuation); and business property is taxed at the highest rates, often with utility property taxed at even higher rates than ordinary businesses *(1987 Census of Govern-*

ments, Appendix A and B; U.S. Advisory Commission 1990, Table 38). In some states, the formal differentials among the classes are small; in others, the differences are very large, as much as a ratio of 5:1 for major classes in New York.[5] Formal classification narrows the tax base in the sense of limiting local governments' ability to fully tax the low-rated types of property, which is not to say that local government officials have been opponents of classification systems.

As noted earlier, owner-occupied residential property received favorable treatment in a number of states more than fifty years ago, in the form of "homestead exemptions," usually by exempting the first thousand dollars of assessed value from tax. If the ratio of assessed to market value for homeowner property is low and the exemption large, the homestead exemption can remove a large fraction of this property from the tax rolls, as has been the case in Louisiana for many years.[6] Homestead exemptions have spread to forty-six states and the District of Columbia. In eighteen of these states, the exemption (in Indiana, it takes the form of a credit) is available to all property owners. In the others, it is restricted to the elderly, the disabled, veterans, and households with low incomes or low house values. In most of the first group of eighteen states, the exemption is larger for one or more of these presumably disadvantaged groups.

Another widespread form of property tax relief for residential property takes the form of rebates or credits against income taxes, based on property tax payments, provided by the state government. In thirty-two states and the District of Columbia, there are state-financed "circuit-breakers"—the amount of the relief is a function both of income and of the relation of the property tax payment to income. In some states, the program applies only to the elderly; where it applies to all ages, it is (like the homestead exemption) usually more generous for the elderly. Some of the all-age programs are very costly: in 1988 Michigan's circuit-breaker payments, for example, were equal to about 10 percent of total property tax revenue and close to 20 percent of the revenue from taxes on residential property (U.S.

Advisory Commission 1990, Table 36; *1987 Census of Governments,* Tables 1 and 4). Paradoxically, the circuit-breaker may act to limit the narrowing of the property tax base—the greater the extent that residential property tax bills are in effect paid from state funds, the less the pressure from homeowners for reducing the taxable value of their property.

An increasing number of states have authorized or directed local governments to provide property tax reductions to foster local economic development, typically in the form of time-limited exemption of some or all new investment in business structures and/or equipment (sometimes called *abatements* because of the supposedly temporary nature of the exemptions).[7] Because the abatements and exemptions take such different forms, there are no national data on the extent of these incentives in the aggregate. However, in a good many cities, especially large cities in the Northeast and Midwest, almost all major nonresidential building projects in the late 1970s and 1980s had some degree of property tax incentive before the project was launched. Of course, in some of these cities, because of the traditional discriminatory practices, the effective rates on newly built commercial structures would have made any investment unprofitable, in the absence of tax breaks.

Another structural change affecting the tax base has been almost entirely involuntary. Around the beginning of this century, state and local governments made a 180-degree turn in their policies toward public utilities and railroads: They had been willing captives of railroad and utility moguls in respect to both regulation and taxation, and they became, in the wake of the progressive movement, exploiters, especially in property taxation. For decades, railroads and utilities were subject to property taxes that were dramatically higher than those on ordinary businesses; sometimes this was explicitly provided by law, but more often it was the result of a combination of formal provision and informal administrative discretion. First, it was generally believed that this was a sure-fire way of exporting part of local tax burdens to residents of other places; and, second, it was also believed that the price elasticity of the local demand for the services produced by these industries was so low that the utilities were neutral and convenient intermediaries in the tax collection process. It should have been obvious decades ago that both propositions were nonsense, but it took ages for that to be understood by economists; some decision-makers still subscribe to the old nonsense.

Thirty years ago, railroads, other major transportation carriers (i.e., airlines, pipelines, and interstate motor carriers), and public utilities accounted for about 13 percent of total property tax revenues; their property tax payments amounted to 6.3 percent of national income originating in the sector, compared to less than 2 percent for other nonfarm business sectors (Netzer 1966). But this has been changing, and rapidly. Economic changes have removed some major segments of the capital stock of this sector from the property tax base: The railroad network has shrunk, especially in those parts of the country where the railroads had been the most overtaxed (the Northeast, in general), and a large amount of telecommunications equipment is now owned by customers rather than telephone companies and is either exempt from property taxation entirely or taxed at the lower effective rates characteristic of ordinary businesses. In addition, federal legislation enacted beginning in 1976 now prohibits states from discriminatorily taxing interstate railroads, airlines, and motor carriers, and state tribunals have become less reluctant to intervene against discriminatory taxation of energy and telecommunications utilities.

By the time of the 1987 census of governments, transportation and public utility property accounted for only about 5 percent of the total assessed value of property subject to tax, compared to about 9 percent thirty years earlier. This was mostly a consequence of tax policy, for the value of structures and equipment owned by this sector declined far less as a share of the total value of privately owned structures and equipment over the same years, from 18.5 percent to 14.6 percent. Moreover, most of that relative decline occurred early in the period, when there were few property tax structural changes (Department of Commerce 1987, 1989 tape).[8]

Effects of Changes on Tax Base Composition

The structural changes that effectively narrowed the tax base had contradictory results from the standpoint of the before-and-after composition of the tax base. Progressively exempting more business personal property, restricting the taxation of farmland, reluctantly changing the property tax treatment of transportation and public utility companies, and offering all sorts of economic development incentives can reduce the nonresidential share of the tax base. But classification and homestead exemptions will reduce the residential share: the shares of both sectors cannot be reduced simultaneously.

What has been happening, in reality? Residential real property accounted for about 40 percent of taxable property values in 1956, and a slightly larger percentage of property tax revenue (Netzer 1966, chapter 2). Similar calculations for 1966, 1979, and 1981 show a persistent rise in the residential percentage. The *1987 Census of Governments* shows that in 1986 the residential percentage of taxable property values was just over 50, a large increase over the entire period. In part, this does reflect underlying economic trends: The national wealth statistics show that the value of residential structures has been rising somewhat more rapidly than that of private nonresidential structures.

On the other hand, the value of business equipment (equal to that of business structures since about 1980) has been rising substantially more rapidly than the value of either residential or business structures—about 40 percent more rapidly since 1956 and with an even greater disparity in more recent years (U.S. Department of Commerce 1987; Musgrave 1990). The shrinking scope of the taxation of business personal property may be the culprit in the decline in the nonresidential share of the tax base (also, transportation and utilities own a good deal more equipment than structures). But changes in land values also may be a significant explanatory variable. Land is surely a larger share of the total value of residential real property than of business real property. Therefore, if land values rose more rapidly than structure values, which probably is the case, the residential share would have risen, with a constant structure of the property tax. In sum, we really don't know the net contribution of the structural changes in those changes that have occurred in the composition of the tax base.

Ceilings on Tax Rates and Tax Levies

Strictly speaking, the adoption of state restrictions on the overall level of local property taxes is not a structural change that narrows the scope of the tax base, but property tax limitations usually are meant to reduce the ability of local governments to exploit whatever tax base is defined by law—they *are,* effectively, reductions in the tax base. Constitutional limits on local property tax rates go back more than a century, but, with few exceptions, they were readily circumvented. In the past two decades, however, many states have adopted limitations that really bind. One type of effective limitation is setting a ceiling on the amount by which local governments can increase their property tax levies—the total amount they intend to collect from the tax—in any one year, either a prescribed percentage-point increase or a limitation keyed to some external economic indicator. The ceiling cannot be circumvented by increases in the property tax rolls, as was the case for most of the older types of ceilings on property tax rates. Limitations in this form were adopted explicitly to prevent local governments from exploiting reassessments that tracked rising market values, especially in inflationary periods. Thus, such limitations are found mostly in states in which local assessments do a reasonable job of tracking market values, like Minnesota and New Jersey.

Inflation plus good assessment practice (or reforms that promised to improve assessment practices) led, by the late 1970s, to a second form of effective limitation, setting a low ceiling on effective property tax rates, perhaps well below the rates that exist at the time the ceiling is adopted, as in the case of Proposition 13 in California in 1978 and Proposition 2½ in Massachusetts in

1980. In the California case, there is also a drastic limit on increases in the taxable value of properties that do not change
ownership, in effect immunizing an increasing share of the value
of real property from taxation over time. There have been other
types of limitations adopted in the 1970s and 1980s as well,
including restrictions on the rate at which assessments can be
increased (regardless of market values) in states where local politics tends to focus on nominal tax rates.

Structural Change in Places with Economic Distress

It can be argued that most of the important structural changes in the
property tax during the 1970s and 1980s were political responses to
rapid growth and inflation in prosperous states and parts of states,
which tended to produce rapid increases in taxable property values,
thus making it easy for officials to satisfy the demands for public
services associated with rapid growth by increasing property tax
revenues without increasing published tax rates. This enraged both
those whose current incomes had kept pace with growth and inflation and those whose current incomes had not but who had substantial unrealized capital gains on their real property. But the
narrowing of the tax base and limitations on tax rates and levies also
affected places in which economic and population decline, not
growth, was the rule. Economic trends had spectacular effects on
the market value of real property, the bulk of the property tax base,
effects that tended to be exacerbated in the case of declining cities
by the changes in the structure of the property tax.

This is shown in Table 3.4 for most of the large central cities
of the country, divided in the table into Frostbelt and Sunbelt
cities, for the 1966–81 period. The table covers all the cities for
which the requisite *Census of Governments* data are available; it
stops in 1981 because the *1987 Census of Governments* contains
no data on market value, only assessed value. The first column
shows the effects of economic change alone; property values in
constant dollars decreased sharply in a good many of the
Frostbelt cities and increased sharply in most of the Sunbelt cities,

Table 3.4

Percent Change in Property Values, in Constant Dollars, Large "Frostbelt" and "Sunbelt" Cities, 1966–81[a]

City	Percent change in market value of real property[b]	Percent change in taxable property value base[c]	Exhibit: Percent change in personal income in constant dollars[d]
Detroit	−64.3	66.1	[−18.9]
Cleveland	−47.9	N.A.	[−8.3]
St. Louis	−34.9	−40.5	−26.0
Newark	−34.3	−39.0	[−9.7]
Buffalo	−25.8	−24.0	[−2.3]
Pittsburgh	−17.0	−17.0	[5.5]
New York	−8.6	−9.7	−11.6
Milwaukee	−3.4	−15.2	[−0.5]
Cincinnati	−3.1	N.A.	[6.2]
Philadelphia	−1.3	−1.3	−11.3
Boston	−0.1	−0.4	−4.9
Baltimore	4.5	−16.0	−13.8
Toledo	8.9	N.A.	[6.6]
Minneapolis	9.1	−4.1	[23.5]
Indianapolis	14.1	3.8	[4.6]
Chicago	21.0	−12.2	[−0.8]
Columbus	45.7	N.A.	[27.3]
New Orleans	17.3	−6.9	5.5
Atlanta	54.3	18.7	[18.0]
Jacksonville	56.3	71.7	37.7
Oklahoma City	57.8	53.4	[58.4]
Nashville	83.4	62.2	28.0
Portland	93.9	101.7	[67.0]
Baton Rouge	102.9	20.1	02.0
Denver	113.4	77.0	22.7
Tulsa	120.4	118.7	[65.9]
Albuquerque	132.4	132.2	[66.6]
Memphis	145.1	46.0	[35.5]
Honolulu	151.6	153.7	51.2
Charlotte	191.5	191.8	[44.5]
Phoenix	397.3	326.8	[123.3]

[a]The Frostbelt cities in the top half of the table include seventeen of the nineteen cities in the Northeast and Midwest with a 1980 population of 300,000 or more. The Sunbelt cities include fourteen of the thirty cities in the South and West with a 1980 population of 300,000 or more. The excluded cities are: (a) cities for which the requisite data are not available (usually because assessed value data are published in the *Census of Governments* only for whole counties, true for all cities in Texas); (b) all cities in California, because of the effect of Proposition 13 on assessed values; and (c) Washington, D.C.

Table 3.4 *(continued)*

bBased on data from Volume 2 of the *Census of Governments* for 1967 and 1982. Market value estimates are based on the gross assessed value of locally assessed real property divided by the weighted average ratio of assessed values to actual prices of a sample of properties sold, for "ordinary real estate" in 1966 and for "measurable sales of all use categories" in 1981. The percentage change in market value so estimated was divided by the change in the implicit price deflator for state and local governments between 1966 and 1981, from the National Income and Product Accounts. Because there are partial exemptions of certain types of property in some of the cities, these estimates are not precise measures of the change in the constant dollar market value of real property actually subject to tax.

cThese estimates take into account changes in provisions for partial exemptions, as well as changes in the coverage of other components of the property tax, notably locally assessed "personal" property (largely business machinery, inventories, and motor vehicles, with major variations in coverage among the states) and property (mostly public utility and mining property) assessed by state government agencies. In essence, such changes are treated as exogenous to the city government, while changes in the way in which real property is assessed by local assessing officers are treated as endogenous. The figures in this column indicate how the tax base would have changed if local assessment practices in 1981 were similar to those in 1966, but with the actual changes in market value of real property, exemptions, and coverage of the property tax. The deflator described in note b was applied here. The *1982 Census of Governments* does not provide data on assessed values of personal and state-assessed property below the county level for Ohio; no estimates can be made for Ohio cities.

dPersonal income estimates in current dollars, from the Bureau of Economic Analysis, U.S. Department of Commerce, deflated as described in note b. Personal income data are available only for counties and for cities that are co-extensive with counties or are independent of counties. The figures in brackets are for entire counties that include suburban territory as well as the city; because population suburbanized during this period, the bracketed figures in most cases understate the declines in real income or overstate the increases actually experienced in the central city itself.

---

and the percentage changes were a good deal larger than those in per capita income. The second column shows the changes in the taxable property tax base (excluding changes that were solely a result of differences in assessment administration practices). In all of the Frostbelt cities in the table for which data are available, the taxable property tax base declined in real terms, except for Indianapolis, which had a small increase. If we had data for 1991, it is probable that we would note that the declines in the taxable property tax base had been reversed in some, but not all, northeastern cities, but had continued in most of the midwestern cities. So, it should be no surprise that fiscal crisis has become a more or less permanent state of affairs for a good many large cities, with huge shrinkage in the property tax base and little hope of rescue from the outside in the form of major increases in state and federal aid.

Journalists will see the dramatic numbers in Table 3.4 in terms of physically devastated neighborhoods, the acres of abandonment in residential areas of Detroit, the legendary South Bronx, and boarded-up stores and older office buildings in central business districts. In fact, Detroit aside, physical abandonment was largely a phenomenon of the 1966–76 period, with a fair amount of subsidized rebuilding since then. However, much of the new investment did not go onto the property tax rolls because of various exemptions and abatements. The economist's explanation for the severity of the decline in the property tax base in Frostbelt cities (and the corresponding rapidity of the increase in Sunbelt cities) lies in the magnified effect of decline and expansion on land values, which have been close to zero, or even negative, in large sections of the Detroits. Even in the Frostbelt cities that were prosperous in the 1980s, land values in constant dollars seldom rose significantly in large parts of those cities outside the central business district and most desirable gentrified residential areas.

Efficiency and Equity Effects of the Changing Property Tax

One cannot discuss the effects of the property tax without specifying the theoretical basis from which the discussion proceeds, that is, who bears the burden of changes in property taxes. Usually, such discussions are cast in terms of the supposed conflict between the "New View" and the "Traditional View" of the incidence of the tax. That conflict is not a real one, in general and in the specific context of this chapter. In the shortest of short terms, the burden (benefit) from an increase (decrease) in the property tax on a specific asset almost always will be borne by the owner of that asset. In the longest of long terms, when equilibrium has finally been achieved, the burden (benefit) in the main will be diffused among all owners of capital in the form of a reduced rate of return on all types of capital in all locations, that is, in proportion to the amount of capital that each household owns.

In between, in the long period that is truly relevant for policy—and when the policy issue at hand is whether to increase (decrease) the property tax in a particular place, or to narrow or broaden its coverage, or to grant new types of economic development incentives or remove old ones—the burden is borne by or the benefit accrued to the owners of the least mobile factors of production in the places where and in the economic sectors for which the tax changes are being made or contemplated. So reducing the property taxes on business property by exempting inventories from personal property taxation, a popular action in the last two decades, will most benefit owners of in-state businesses whose goods and services compete least with the output of firms in other states (like most retailers and producers of consumer services), the least skilled (and therefore least mobile) employees of those businesses, the owners of the land and structures occupied by those businesses, and the purchasers of their goods and services who themselves are not especially mobile geographically. The reverse is true for business property tax increases, in both cases framing the issue as increases or decreases relative to the actions that other states are taking at the same time.

The fact that the ultimate burden or benefit from a property tax change in one state or city accrues to immobile local factors of production and immobile local households does not mean that everyone else is indifferent to the economic processes through which these effects are realized over time. Immobile factors and households benefit from tax reductions as capital is attracted to the city or state and employment, income, sales, and asset values rise. As with economic growth triggered by any other cause, there are a few losers from the process, but mostly winners—and the enterprises and people who are attracted to the area are likely to see themselves as winners, even if we economists do not.

A similar situation exists with regard to changes in property tax on residential property in a state or city. Because the structures and, especially, the land are less mobile than their occupants, the burden or benefit accrues mainly to the owners of the land and structures. For owner-occupied housing, there is, of course, no distinction between the two economic roles. For renter-occupied housing, some of the burden or benefit will accrue to tenants, because some of them are quite immobile geographically—but many are not, over time.

These probable outcomes suggest that reduced reliance on the property tax is likely to be a popular course of action, in the future as it has been in the past. Is this a good thing, compared to the conceivable alternatives, which are higher local government expenditures or other types of local government revenue? What is right and wrong about a tax that has become one largely on the value of housing, public utility property, commercial and industrial structures built before the era of generous tax incentives for new investment, and—in some states—motor vehicles?

(1) Equity: A reduced role for the property tax in a given city or state will have mixed income distribution effects, assuming that the reductions are across the board. Relatively low-income people will benefit as immobile workers in local establishments, immobile consumers, and immobile tenants. But relatively high-income people also will benefit as landowners, newspaper proprietors and owners of television stations, managers and shareholders of local utilities, and so on. The best evidence on the income-elasticity of demand for owner-occupied housing suggests that it is fairly low, so reductions in local taxes on owner-occupied housing should benefit low-income homeowners disproportionately.

(2) Another consideration in actual decision making, and one that has been held to be a virtue in regard to the "fiscal health" of cities by some economists (Ladd and Yinger 1989), is the extent to which the tax burden can be exported. Superficially, given that business property is ordinarily a large component of the tax base in central cities, it appears that the property tax should be the preferred revenue instrument on this score. However, as my anal-

ysis of incidence above suggests, I am skeptical about the exportability of the business property tax except in the very long run. Therefore, a reduction in the use of this tax in one city should not make its tax burden less exportable in any significant way. As Ladd and Yinger suggest, the local tax that may be the most exportable of all is a city earnings tax on nonresident commuters, whose status as earners in the city is likely to be a relatively immobile one.

(3) The other side of that coin is the effect of the level of the property tax on new investment in that city, obviously of special concern to cities that are not in good economic health. If the burdens and benefits of property tax differentials (or increases/decreases) are not very exportable, that means that local people and enterprises will gain from tax reductions. The mechanism by which they benefit is the inflow of capital, that is, economic development. Indeed, it may not matter much whether the taxes are reduced on a targeted basis or across the board, from the standpoint of economic development over time. Because the property tax is one that is measured by the value of capital, its reduction should be more beneficial to local economic growth than reductions in local sales and income taxes.[9] On the other hand, a considerable portion of the tax base consists of the value of land itself; reducing taxes on land values has no effect other than to make the present owners of that land richer.

(4) It does seem likely that lower property taxes would have positive effects on the quality of the housing stock, in particular the rental housing stock. However, the price effects in this sector are likely to be more important than the quality effects because at the lower end of the rental housing market both the price and the income elasticity of demand for quality appears to be very low.

(5) Stability of the tax base: The data in Table 3.4 suggest that the market value of taxable property may be an exceedingly unsafe tax base for very poor cities, far more so than alternative tax bases, like income. Stability aside, there is real question about the adequacy of a property tax largely on housing in very poor cities, the value of which may be lower relatively than personal

incomes. A few years ago, in connection with school finance litigation in New Jersey, I calculated the value of residential property in a number of the poorest cities in the state, which had lost much of their business tax base over the years.[10] In Camden, New Jersey, the mean value per housing unit in 1981 was about $6,000, less than a tenth of the statewide average!

(6) The property tax has a very long history of being inexpensively but very poorly administered, because of the difficulty of valuing real property and both discovering and valuing personal property, and because of populist opposition to effective administration even when technically feasible. The narrowing of the tax base, along with technological improvements, has made the tax far less difficult to administer, provided money is spent to do so (like for auditing business personal property tax returns, which is a startlingly uncommon practice), so that it really is no longer correct to praise reduced reliance on the property tax as substituting inherently easy-to-administer taxes for an inherently difficult-to-administer tax.[11]

(7) Frequently, the property tax has been denounced from the standpoint of the disparities in the taxable capacity of local jurisdictions. But this, of course, is true of any local tax. If public services are to be financed largely from local revenues, there will be interjurisdictional disparities.

Most urban economists agree on what would be the best of all possible revenue systems for cities: taxes on the value of land to finance public goods and the external benefits from publicly provided private goods and marginal-cost-based user charges for everything else. But of course, the property tax we do have is not a land value tax. Nonetheless, the theoretical prescription tells us something about the conceptual advantages and disadvantages of the actual real-world property tax vis-à-vis actual real-world alternatives. The fact that land value is an important component of the property tax base is, as the above discussion makes clear, a major factor in the evaluation of the tax. The inclusion of land makes the tax better in most respects, and, therefore, makes the case for less reliance on it weaker on both equity and efficiency grounds. On the other hand, the property tax is an exceedingly inept user charge, and therefore should be replaced, for the financing of private goods, by properly designed user charges, as economists never tire of saying.

Future Prospects

There is no reason to expect that, in the foreseeable future, the property tax will be displaced in local finance by a substantial increase in the role of federal and state aid to local governments, as occurred in the 1930s and again in the 1960s and 1970s. No doubt, in some states, there will be major reforms in school finance, leading to more state financing of the schools. Also, reforms in the health-care finance system may marginally reduce local government spending for hospitals, in some places. But even these important policy shifts will not amount to a major shift in intergovernmental fiscal relations in this country.

The rapid decline in the importance of the property tax from the mid-1960s to the late 1970s was not solely caused by the changes in the intergovernmental fiscal system during those years. In addition, there was the widespread perception, right or wrong, that the property tax is inequitable, along several dimensions, relative to plausible alternatives. It is not obvious that this remains the dominant perception or is seen as a particularly urgent policy concern. Perhaps as important in explaining the major role of voter- and legislature-generated property tax ceilings and caps—on rates, assessments, and levies, sometimes done indirectly via classification schemes—in the decline of the property tax was the rapidity of the increases in the value of owner-occupied housing, especially in places where assessments did track market values reasonably well (and also in places where there were threats that assessments might do so in the near future). House values rose rapidly because of inflation in general and the existence of negative real mortgage interest rates; both are conditions that are unlikely to return soon. If house prices do not increase rapidly, a new wave of Proposition 13s is most unlikely.

On the other hand, huge declines in housing values can lead, as they did in the Great Depression, to strong reactions against the property tax (in the 1930s, Florida voters nearly approved a referendum proposal to abolish the tax entirely) if assessed values do not decline commensurately. But there is no reason to expect that scenario to be played out on a national basis.

Conceivably, however, there could be new rounds of the experience depicted in Table 3.1, collapsing property values in major Frostbelt cities. However, it is implausible to assume that the 1989–92 difficulties in real estate markets, notably the high vacancies in commercial property and the sharp decline in sales and prices in the upper part of the residential market, represent some fundamental change, and that we should expect perpetual low values, even perpetually declining values in constant dollars as our future, in a large number of cities. It is true that, in the worst of cases—as in the Table 3.4 worst cases—substantial declines in the property tax base in real terms will aggravate difficult social and fiscal problems, with large increases in central city tax rates on any property that remains taxable and massive capital losses. But that need not be the universal experience even of Frostbelt cities, any more than it was in the late 1960s and 1970s.

Thus, circumstances that will lead to wholesale replacement of the property tax do not seem likely, in the near-to-intermediate future. Nor *should* the property tax be replaced wholesale in the light of its relative strengths and weaknesses.

Conclusion

Just over thirty-five years ago, a public finance economist who is now largely unknown but who then was regarded as one of the most perceptive analysts and practitioners in the field, George W. Mitchell, forecast that in twenty years, "the property tax will . . . have become an all-but-forgotten relic of an earlier fiscal age" (Mitchell 1956, 494), that is, it would renew its decline as a source of local government revenue.[12] The decline did start once more a few years later, but stopped. About a decade ago, I revisited the Mitchell forecast and concluded that during the 1980s some decline but not much was likely. That is also my forecast for the 1990s. For good and bad reasons, decision-makers (including the voters in occasional referenda) will chip away at the coverage of the tax, offer more incentives and preferences, cap rates and levies, and increase the use of local nonproperty taxes and user charges. But without major changes in fiscal federalism in the shape of shifting financing responsibilities for local public services to the higher levels of government, the overall role of the property tax will change little.

Notes

1. "General revenue" rather than total revenue is used in Table 3.2 because the data by type of local government are readily available only for general revenue. The main difference is that general revenue excludes water, electric power, gas, and transit utility revenue.
2. The denominator of the measure used is total state-local tax revenue in order to avoid distortions due solely to decisions concerning the locus of the administrative responsibility for functions that are largely financed by the state governments.
3. The diversity in fiscal institutions within the American system of fiscal federalism in general is not easy to explain: In a related paper, I tried to explain interstate differences in reliance on user charges without much success (Netzer 1991).
4. In Wisconsin, the "State legislature has elected to provide owners of farmland subject to agricultural use restrictions with income tax credits and refunds rather than use-based assessments" *(1987 Census of Governments,* Appendix C).
5. There are even larger differentials among classes of personal property in some states, but the classes with the very low rates are small ones. The large differential for New York is the combined result of a number of formally discriminating provisions, rather than a single explicit provision; however, it is obvious to this observer that the legislature has been entirely aware of the combined effect from the time the classification system was enacted in 1981.
6. As of 1986, the gross assessed value of single-family houses (rented or owner-occupied) in that state was $4,858 million. The total amount of the homestead exemptions was $4,040 million *(1987 Census of Governments,* Tables 2 and 4). Some single-family houses were rented, not owner-occupied, so it is likely that the exemption removed more than 90 percent of the gross assessed value of single-family owner-occupied houses from taxation.

7. Substantively, this was not entirely a new thing. Extralegal informal drastic underassessment of industrial property had been the rule in most medium-sized and small cities in the United States for decades, especially in regions that early on were aggressive competitors for industry (the South in general) and in places where the dominant local industries had been declining. But few large cities had been participants in this until recently, and the conversion of the practice from informal to formal surely increased its impact in other places.

8. This last set of calculations ignores land values, which is part of the reason why the Department of Commerce wealth data do not match the tax roll data even approximately.

9. An exception may be the reduction of taxes on selected business inputs like utility services (or some other business purchases covered by the general sales tax), which could be strategic for the industries that are closest to the margin with respect to choosing whether or not to locate in that city (e.g., telecommunications services for financial services companies).

10. The case was *Abbot v. Burke,* decided by the New Jersey Supreme Court in favor of the plaintiffs, who were residents of a number of the state's poor cities.

11. Besides, one substitute for the property tax, more reliance on user charges, involves revenue instruments that are indeed difficult to administer.

12. Mitchell at that time was the vice president in charge of research at the Federal Reserve Bank of Chicago. A student of Frank Knight, Henry Simons, and Simeon Leland at the University of Chicago, he had been director of research for the Illinois Tax Commission (and a member of the commission), director of studies for Congressional committees, and Illinois finance director during the administration of Adlai Stevenson. In 1961, he became President Kennedy's first appointee to the Federal Reserve Board and later became vice chairman of the board. He retired in 1975.

References

Ladd, Helen F., and Yinger, John. 1989. *America's Ailing Cities.* Baltimore: Johns Hopkins University Press.

Mitchell, George W. 1956. "Is This Where We Came In?" In *Proceedings of the Forty-Ninth Annual Conference on Taxation,* National Tax Association.

Musgrave, John C. 1990. "Fixed Reproducible Tangible Wealth in the United States, 1982–89." *Survey of Current Business (September): 99–106.*

Netzer, Dick. 1966. *Economics of the Property Tax.* Washington, D.C.: The Brookings Institution.

Netzer, Dick. 1991. "Differences in Reliance on User Charges by American State and Local Governments." Paper presented at the annual research conference of the Committee on Taxation, Resources and Economic Development, Cambridge, Massachusetts. The conference papers are to be published in a special issue of the *Public Finance Quarterly* in 1992.

U.S. Advisory Commission on Intergovernmental Relations. 1990. *Significant Features of Fiscal Federalism*, Volume 1, *Budget Processes and Tax Systems*.

U.S. Department of Commerce, Bureau of the Census. 1989. *1987 Census of Governments*. Volume 2, *Taxable Property Values*. Washington: Government Printing Office.

U.S. Department of Commerce, Bureau of Economic Analysis. 1987. *Fixed Reproducible Tangible Wealth in the United States, 1925–85*. Washington, D.C.: Government Printing Office.

U.S. Department of Commerce, Bureau of Economic Analysis. 1989. *National Wealth Tape*. Computer tape sold through Atlanta office of BEA.

4

The Outlook for Owner-Occupied Housing in the Year 2000

JAMES R. FOLLAIN

Introduction

The economic fortunes of many participants in the U.S. economy are sensitive to changes in the value of the owner-occupied housing stock. Individual owner-occupants are sensitive because housing is usually the most valuable asset in their portfolios. Residential structures represent about 25 percent of the value of all assets in the United States (Federal Reserve System 1991, 5, Table 1). The local government sector is also sensitive because property tax revenues are directly related to the value of the housing stock. Local governments collected about $50 billion from the property tax on owner-occupied housing in 1987 (Peters 1988). Businesses that help households preserve and enhance the value of owner-occupied housing arc also affected. The gross housing product in 1989 was $440 billion, which is largely made up of nonfarm owner-occupied housing and represents about 9 percent of GNP (U.S. Department of Commerce 1991, 724, Table 1279).

The value of the stock of owner-occupied housing, exclusive of land, is estimated to be about $4.5 trillion. The value of the land upon which this housing sits is probably worth another trillion dollars.[1] The value of the stock, exclusive of land, increased by about 23 percent in real terms during the 1980s and by over 30 percent in the 1970s.

What can we expect to happen between now and the year 2000 to the value of this important asset? Some argue that housing values are likely to decline substantially during the 1990s. One twosome has been particularly pessimistic. Greg Mankiw and David Weil (1989) estimate that the real price of housing may decline by as much as 47 percent between now and 2010. If this dire forecast proves to be even remotely close to the truth, the many people who rely upon this asset are likely to experience dark days ahead. For a variety of reasons that are set forth below, such a pervasive decline for the entire country is quite unlikely and would come as a surprise to me and some other housing economists.[2]

My best guess is that the value of the owner-occupied housing stock will increase in excess of 25 percent in real terms during the 1990s and possibly more. Such an increase would make the 1990s a better decade for owner-occupied housing than the 1980s but would fall far short of the 30 percent real increase experienced in the 1970s. The estimate is based upon a relatively simple model of the housing market and is subject to numerous caveats and assumptions regarding growth in the economy. Alternative estimates are provided for best- and worst-case scenarios. Despite the simplicity of the model, the exercise and the discussion of the model shed light upon the determinants of the value of the housing stock and the controversial aspects of the forecast on which housing economists may disagree.

The Market for Owner-Occupied Housing: Model, Trends, and Areas of Controversy

The nominal value of the nonfarm owner-occupied housing stock, exclusive of land, was about $3.56 trillion in 1990, up from $2.1 trillion in 1980 and $575 billion in 1970. The respective real values of the stock (in 1987 dollars) for these three years are: $3.26 trillion (1990), $2.56 trillion (1980), and $1.83 trillion (1970). (See Musgrave 1992, Tables 10 and 12.) The largest absolute increases took place in 1977 and 1978, when over $213 billion was added to the stock of owner-occupied housing. This section of the chapter explores factors that generate changes in this measure of the stock of owner-occupied housing.

The model of the housing market employed in this analysis begins with the decomposition of the value of the owner-occupied housing stock into three components: $KOWN = KHH * P * HO$ where $KOWN$ is the real aggregate value of the stock of owner-occupied housing; KHH is the value of stock of housing per owner household; P is the price of a typical and constant quality unit; and HO is the number of households that own their homes. The discussion below focuses on each of the components of $KOWN$ and behavioral equations that describe the behavior of each component of $KOWN$. The discussion also examines recent trends in the components and the areas of controversy among housing economists.

Before the discussion of the model begins, it is useful to explain some concepts that are embedded within it. Because housing is a long-lived asset, it is essential to distinguish between the consumption of housing services and the purchase of the stock of housing. At the time a person buys a home, the transaction is best labeled as an investment in a particular asset, housing stock. The transaction changes the household's balance sheet to reflect more housing, less of some other asset (probably a savings account), and, usually, an increase in mortgage debt. During the time after occupancy, it is possible to define the consumption of housing services as the flow of services generated by that house per year. The cost of this consumption of housing services is a function of many variables including the annual cost of debt, the opportunity cost of equity in the house, depreciation and maintenance, plus or minus the effect of homeownership upon the tax liabilities of the household. Recognition of this dual nature of housing—housing is both an investment good and a consumption good—is essential to understanding the market for owner-occupied housing.

Housing Services per Owner Household: KHH

KHH, as measured by the value of the stock of housing (excluding land) per owner household, has grown substantially in nominal dollars, going from about $10,000 in 1964 to over $50,000 in 1989 (Figure 4.1). In real terms, the growth is lower but still substantial; *KHH* grew by 8 percent in the 1970s, by over 10 percent in the 1980s, and by over 30 percent since 1964. The annual growth rates in real housing demand per household fluctuated during the past twenty-five years; they seldom exceeded 1 percent per year, and the largest decline, which occurred in 1982, was no more than 2 percent.

Model

The amount of housing owned by a particular household stems from the household's demand for housing services. Like any demand function, this one depends upon the income of the household and the price of the good relative to other goods. In fact, economists have identified a strong positive link between household permanent income and the demand for housing services. Income elasticity estimates are usually around unity for homeowners.[3]

The role and definition of the price of housing are more complex than for an ordinary consumption good because it must take into account that housing is both a consumption and an investment good. The preferred measure of price for a long-run study of this type is what economists call the real after-tax user cost of capital, which is the annualized cost of owning and using one arbitrary unit of housing stock. User cost for owner-occupants is usually written:

$$UC_0 = (1 - t_y)(i + t_p) + \delta - \pi_e$$

where t_y is the household's marginal federal income tax rate; i is an average of the cost of debt and equity; t_p is the property tax

Figure 4.1. **Trends in the Value of Owner-Occupied Housing per Household (*KHH*)**

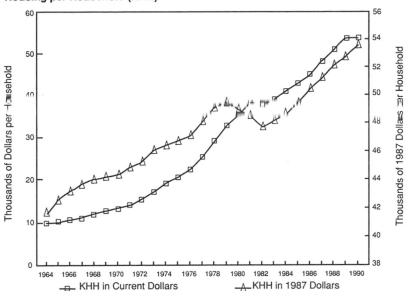

rate; δ is the rate of depreciation; and, π_e is the rate of expected capital gains. This specification captures two key aspects of the cost of housing: (1) owner-occupied is granted substantial tax advantages because imputed rental income is exempt from taxation and mortgage interest is deductible; and (2) appreciation in the asset price of housing should be subtracted from the ongoing or cash outlays for owner-occupied housing to arrive at a true measure of the cost of housing.

The price elasticity of housing demand is defined with reference to the real after-tax user cost of owner-occupied housing *(UC₀)*. Economists are not as much in agreement about the price elasticity of demand as they are about the income elasticity of demand. Empirical estimates can be found above and below unity. An estimate of unity is used below, which seems especially appropriate in a long-run exercise of this type.

The previous discussion can be summarized in the following equation, which indicates the demand for owner-occupied housing per owner household:

$$KHH = \beta_{10} + \beta_{11}Y + \beta_{12}UC_oP$$

where β_{11} and β_{12} are the income and price elasticities of demand, Y is the permanent income of the household; UC_o the user cost of capital expressed as a percent of the real price of housing, P. Percentage changes *(dln)* in *KHH* can be expressed as:

$$dln\ KHH = \beta_{11}dln\ Y + \beta_{12}UC_odln\ P \qquad (1)$$

The income and price elasticities are assumed equal to unity, i.e., $\beta_{11} = 1$ and $\beta_{12} = 1$.

The primary area of controversy surrounding the equation is the distinction between the real and the nominal (expected capital gains excluded) cost of housing. The distinction between these two measures is most pronounced during periods of substantial inflation when nominal interest rates are high relative to real interest rates. In recent years and during the 1960s, these two alternative measures of the cost of housing moved in similar directions; however, they diverged substantially in the very late 1970s when nominal interest rates were increasing while the real after-tax user cost actually declined (see Figure 4.2). Despite this divergence in the late 1970s, most housing economists would agree that the preferred measure of the price of housing for a long-run study of this type is the real after-tax user cost. However, the liquidity constraints faced by many first-time home buyers during periods of high inflation and high nominal interest rates cannot be ignored for short-run analysis. (See also Ling forthcoming.)

Another area of controversy involves the effects of demographic factors such as the age distribution of the population, household composition, and household size upon the household demand for housing. Some efforts have been made to quantify these relationships, most notably by Mankiw and Weil and by Fair and Dominguez; however, economists have not yet produced precise estimates of the effects of these demographic fac-

Figure 4.2. **Trends in User Cost and the Nominal Mortgage Interest Rate**

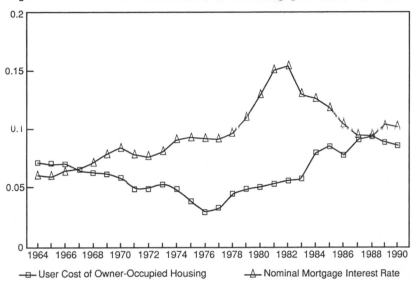

tors upon individual housing demand (Fair and Dominguez 1991).

Asset Price of Owner-Occupied Housing: P

The asset price of owner-occupied housing measures the price or value of a particular amount of housing stock, e.g., price per square foot of housing in a good neighborhood. The Bureau of the Census chooses a new, constant-size, single-family house as its standard of comparison over time and region.[4] The Census price series, which is plotted in Figure 4.3, indicates that the price of its typical unit is about $110,000 in 1990, up from about $22,500 in 1964, about a fivefold increase. The dominant reason for the increase is the increase in the overall rate of inflation, but even in real terms (right axis), the price index shows considerable upward movement. The real price of housing, adjusted by the GDP deflator, is over 20 percent higher than in 1964. The bulk of this increase occurred in the 1970s, when real housing prices increased by over 23 percent. Real housing prices actually de-

clined by over 3 percent during the 1980s despite a rally during
the mid-1980s.

Model

The principal intuition underlying the forces that determine the
market-asset price of housing is as follows. Assume that builders
and developers focus their attention on the gap between the current asset price of housing and the cost of building the unit. If the
gap is positive, then builders have an incentive to construct new
housing and pocket the difference between the asset price and the
cost of construction as their profit. Competition among builders
will eventually force the gap to zero because the additional construction generated by a positive gap will expand the supply of
housing and reduce the asset price needed to clear the market for
owner-occupied housing. The same type of logic applies in reverse when the gap is negative; a negative gap discourages new
construction. If builders are quick to respond to the gap and land
is plentiful, then the asset price of housing will always remain
near its replacement cost. Economists label this situation a perfectly elastic supply of housing, which means that the supply
curve for housing is very flat and equal to the replacement cost of
housing. Such a situation also implies that the asset price of housing is largely unaffected by movements in the demand for
housing.

Herein lies the major area of controversy regarding the supply
of housing: How sensitive is the asset price of housing to shifts in
the demand for housing? Although some evidence exists to suggest that the supply of housing is quite elastic, the evidence is not
ironclad.[5] Furthermore, land is not always plentiful in supply in
many areas and, hence, the price of land may be affected by
movements in the demand for housing. Some, like Muth, myself,
and others, lean toward a situation in which the asset price is
largely unaffected by swings in demand, at least in the medium
and long runs. Others, like Mankiw and Weil, argue that the asset
price is quite sensitive to shifts in the demand for housing.

Figure 4.3. **Trends in the Asset Price of Owner-Occupied Housing (P)**

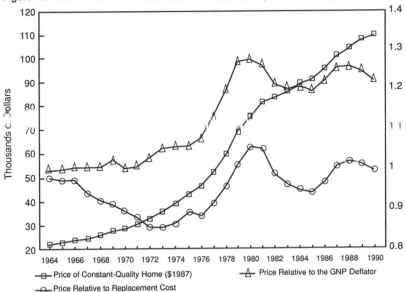

An equation that captures this intuition and controversy can be expressed in logarithmic differentials as follows:

$$dln\ P = \beta_{21}\ dln\ PRC + \beta_{22}\ dln\ KHH*HO \qquad (2)$$

where P is the asset price of housing; PRC is the index of replacement cost; HO is the number of households who own their homes; and β_{21} and β_{22} are parameters. If β_{21} is unity and β_{22} is zero, then the model reduces to the case of a perfectly elastic supply curve. If β_{22} is positive, then an inelastic supply curve holds. Forecasts are provided for cases in which β_{22} is unity and β_{22} equals either .1 or 1.0 (worst-case scenario).

Number of Owner-Occupied Households: HO

The final component in $KOWN$ is the number of owner-occupied households. This series, which is plotted in Figure 4.4, shows considerable and steady growth during the past twenty-five years. The number of owner-occupied households stands at just over sixty million, up about 75 percent since 1964. Only about one-third of this is a result of the increase in the population. Another important reason for the increase is a reduction in average household size from 3.33 to 2.67 persons per household. A rise in the homeownership rate of .75 percent also contributed, but the increase in the homeownership rate has not been steady. Indeed, the aggregate homeownership rate declined during the 1980s (see Figure 4.4).[6]

Model

In my judgment, a model of the number of owner-occupied households is the most difficult to develop and the one on which economists have made the least progress. The principal problem is that the number of owner-occupied households is, like the value of the owner-occupied housing stock, the product of two largely independent forces: the decision to own and the decision to form an independent household. Economists have studied the first of these issues in some detail, but work on the latter question is less far along.[7] What follows is my own relatively simple formulation of an equation that incorporates results of the academic literature on the subject.

The definition of the number of owner-occupied households is a useful place to begin this discussion:

$$dHO = \sum_{i=1}^{K} n_1 hd_i \, ho_i \, (Y, p_o/p_r) \, POP$$

where K is the number of age categories; n_i is the share of the population in the ith age group; hd_i is the household headship rate in the ith age group; ho_i is the fraction of households in the ith age group who own their homes, which depends upon income *(Y)* and the relative price of owning versus renting (p_o/p_r); and *POP* is the size of the total population.

Figure 4.4. **Trends in the Number of Owner-Occupied Households (HO)**

—□— Number of Owner Households (Left)   —△— Home Ownership Rate (Right)

This expression suggests several factors that influence the growth in *HO*. The first and most important is the growth in the size of the population, which is expected to grow by another eighteen million people or so in the next ten years. If the average household size and the aggregate homeownership rate remain constant during the 1990s, then the number of owner-occupied households will increase in proportion to the population increase. Alternatively stated, the elasticity of *HO* with respect to *POP* equals unity, holding fixed a variety of other factors that influence the homeownership rate and the headship rate.

Of course, changes in the rate of homeownership and the headship rate are possible and likely. Although changes in the headship rate have taken place and will probably continue to change, the headship rate has not been studied to the extent that the homeownership decision has been. As a result, this chapter focuses on factors likely to change the preference for homeownership.

One factor that will surely affect future trends in the homeownership rate is the change in the age distribution of the population. We will become an older population in the next ten years. In particular, growth is expected among the forty-five–sixty-four age group relative to the twenty-five–thirty-four age group; note the projected trends in Figure 4.5. Because the homeownership rate is higher for the older age groups than for the younger age groups, the number of owner-occupied households will likely increase during the 1990s even if the homeownership rates within each age group remain constant. A precise estimate of the effect of this aging of the population upon the number of homeowners is difficult to obtain; the forecasts below assume an elasticity of *HO* with respect to the percent of the population, in the age category forty-five–sixty-four is .33.[8]

The homeownership rates among age groups may also change during the 1990s, especially if income and the relative price of owning versus renting change. In fact, the responsiveness of these homeownership rates to changes in income and the relative price of owning versus renting is an important adjustment mechanism incorporated into the model. All else being equal, an increase in income increases the demand for housing per household *(KHH)* and the number of owner-occupied households *(HO)*. These increases, in turn, place upward pressure on the asset price of housing, which reduces *KHH* and *HO*. The model incorporates this type of simultaneity by assuming nonzero income and price elasticities in the equation for *HO*. The income and price elasticities of the demand for owner-occupied housing are assumed to equal .5 and –.5, respectively.

A simple behavioral relationship that captures these varied effects can be summarized as:

$$dln\ HO = \beta_{31}\ dln\ Y + \beta_{32}\ dln\ \frac{UC}{R} +$$

$$\beta_{33}\ dln\ POP + \beta_{34}\ dln\ AGE4564 \qquad (3)$$

where *POP* is the total population of the economy; *R* is the index

Figure 4.5. **Trends in the Distribution of the Population by Age**

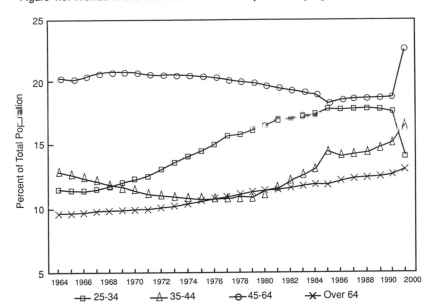

of the price of rental housing; and *AGE4564* is the number of people between the ages of forty-five and sixty-four. $ß_{31}$ and $ß_{32}$ equal .5 and –.5, respectively; $ß_{33}$ equals unity; and $ß_{34}$ equals .33.

The main controversy surrounding this equation involves its parameterization. Economists have not reached the same degree of consensus regarding this equation as they have regarding the demand for housing per household. Although the numbers assumed in the specification above do bear a loose resemblance to the literature and, in my opinion, can be justified as reasonable guesses, they are not offered with a large amount of confidence. Furthermore, the specification omits one other possibly important behavioral response; headship rates (the inverse of household size) may change during the 1990s and may themselves be part of a more complex relationship that involves household income and the relative price of owning and renting. More research on all of these topics is needed to improve the type of forecast offered below

Mankiw-Weil Argument

The complete specification of the model allows the thrust of the Mankiw-Weil argument to be more clearly understood. All else being equal, they argue that an increase in the demand for owner-occupied housing, especially in the late 1970s, was brought about, in large part, by changes in the age distribution of the population (see Figure 4.5). The increase in the size of the home-buying population increased the number of owner-occupied households and, possibly, the demand for housing per household. These increases, in turn, produced higher asset prices for owner-occupied housing, especially in the late 1970s, because the supply of housing in their model for the short- and medium-term horizons is not perfectly elastic, i.e., $ß_2$ is substantially above unity.[9] Population forecasts for the 1990s and the early part of the twenty-first century indicate that the segments responsible for the home-buying boom of the 1970s and 1980s will decline substantially. As they do, demand will diminish, and housing prices will fall substantially.

Forecasts of Owner-Occupied Housing Stock in the Year 2000

Equations 1, 2, and 3 comprise the basis of the forecasts reported in this section. The three endogenous variables are *KHH, P,* and *HO.* The change in the value of the owner-occupied housing stock— *KOWN*—is given as the product of these three variables. These are simultaneously determined by the six exogenous variables of the system: *Y, UC_o, PRC, R, POP,* and *AGE4564.* Three sets of forecasts are reported: the base case, the best case, and the worst case.

Base Case

The key assumptions pertain to the changes expected in the six exogenous variables. Population is expected to increase by 7.2 percent to 268.75 million people, and the percent of the population between forty-five and sixty-four years of age is expected to increase from 29 to 31.8 percent during the decade. Real income is assumed to grow 14 percent during the decade. This is down from the 18 percent growth during the 1980s and the 16 percent during the 1970s. The base case assumes no change in the relative price of owning versus renting and a 5 percent increase in real replacement cost, which is consistent with the idea that the supply of housing will be more hindered in the 1990s by zoning issues, environmental concerns, and limited availability of land than it has been in the past. The results of the base-case forecast, which are contained in Table 4.1, indicate a 31.2 percent increase in the real value of the owner-occupied housing stock *(KOWN)*. *KHH* increases at 6.7 percent. This is less than the increase in real income (14 percent) because the 7.3 percent rise in real housing prices reduces the response of *KHH* to higher income. Most of the rise in *P* is generated by a 5 percent increase in replacement cost and the remainder due to a 24.0 (6.7 + 17.3) percent increase in housing demand, i.e., the sum of the percentage changes in *KHH* and *HO*. The surge in housing demand is generated by a 17.3 percent increase in the number of owner-occupied households, most of which is generated by an increase in the population by over eighteen million households.

The key result is an increase in the value of the owner-occupied housing stock to $7.38 trillion. The result is obtained in this highly stylized model because both real income and population growth are expected to be positive. Given the assumption of a nearly perfectly elastic supply of housing, growth in the value of the stock must occur if the principal determinants of housing demand—income and population growth—grow. As promised in the introduction, this forecast is considerably more optimistic than is the Mankiw-Weil forecast even though it assumes a slowdown in economic growth relative to the previous two decades.

Best Case

An even more optimistic forecast can be generated with a few changes in assumptions. This best-case scenario assumes a

Table 4.1

Base-Case Forecasts

	1990	2000	Base-Case Change (in percent)
KOWN ($Billions)	5, 400.00	7, 380.00	0.312
KHH ($Thousands)	90.00	96.24	0.067
P ($Thousands)	120.00	129.06	0.073
H ($Thousands)	60, 000.00	71, 305.00	0.173
Y ($Thousands)	50.00	57.50	0.140
UC (Rate)	0.10	0.10	0.000
PRC ($Thousands)	120.00	126.00	0.049
R (Rate)	0.10	0.10	0.000
POP (Millions)	250.00	268.75	0.072
AGE 45–64 (in percent)	0.290	0.318	0.092

higher rate of growth in income (16.6 percent), no growth in replacement cost, and a 9.5 percent increase in the cost of rental housing (see Table 4.2). This last assumption reflects the belief that the full effects of the Tax Reform Act of 1986 have yet to be felt on the rental housing market and that the 10 percent or more increase predicted by several economists will be realized in the 1990s (Follain, Hendershott, and Ling 1987).

The increase in *KOWN* is now 37.5 percent, rising to nearly $7.9 trillion in the year 2000. *KHH* increases by 12.9 percent and the number of owner-occupied households by over 23 percent, which reflects the impact of rising income on the number of owner-occupied households. The asset price of housing rises by 3.6 percent, even though replacement cost does not rise because the supply elasticity is positive, though small, in this model.

Worst Case

Of course, a worst-case scenario can also be depicted, using less optimistic assumptions about some of the exogenous variables, as well as a couple of changes in the parameters of the model (see

Table 4.2

Best-Case Assumptions

	1990	2000	Best-Case Change (in percent)	Base-Case Change (in percent)
KOWN ($Billions)	5,400.00	8,045.00	0.375	0.312
KHH ($Thousands)	90.00	102.42	0.129	0.067
P ($Thousands)	120.00	121.43	0.036	0.073
H ($Thousands)	60,000.00	75,754.00	0.233	0.173
Y ($Thousands)	50.00	59.00	0.166	0.140
UC (Rate)	0.10	0.10	0.000	0.000
PRC ($Thousands)	120.00	120.00	0.000	0.049
R (Rate)	0.10	0.11	0.095	0.000
POP (Millions)	250.00	268.75	0.072	0.072
AGE 45–64 (in percent)	0.290	0.318	0.092	0.092

Table 4.3). Income growth is limited to only 4.9 percent, which is characteristic of the slow growth of the late 1980s and early 1990s. Replacement cost is expected to decline by 5.1 percent. This may occur if land prices decline substantially during the 1990s in light of slower projected economic and population growth. The user cost of owner-occupied housing is predicted to increase by 9.5 percent. One justification for this assumption is a reduction in inflationary expectations regarding housing prices during the 1990s, which will increase user cost.[10] Another possible source of upward pressure on user cost in the 1990s is the reduced value of the mortgage interest deduction for many middle-income households.[11]

Two parameters of the model are also changed. The supply elasticity is increased to unity, which generates larger effects upon the asset price of housing, all else being equal. Furthermore, the effect of an increase in the age of the population upon the number of owner-occupied households is reduced to .25 from .33. This is a somewhat arbitrary reduction to reflect the possibility that homeownership rates among age groups have been declining during most of the 1980s and may continue to decline in the 1990s.

Table 4.3

Worst-Case Assumptions

	1990	2000	Worst-Case Change (in percent)	Base-Case Change (in percent)
KOWN ($Billions)	5,400.00	5,540.00	0.026	0.312
KHH ($Thousands)	90.00	87.02	−0.034	0.067
P ($Thousands)	120.00	118.47	−0.013	0.073
H ($Thousands)	60,000.00	64,486.00	0.072	0.173
Y ($Thousands)	50.00	52.50	0.049	0.140
UC (Rate)	0.10	0.11	0.095	0.000
PRC ($Thousands)	120.00	114.00	−0.051	0.049
R (Rate)	0.10	0.10	0.000	0.000
POP (Millions)	250.00	268.75	0.072	0.072
AGE 45–64 (in percent)	0.290	0.318	0.092	0.092

The worst-case scenario certainly does generate a less optimistic forecast, though nothing like the Mankiw-Weil forecast. The value of the stock still increases, though by a small amount, but the asset price of housing declines by 1.3 percent. A steeper decline is not generated because the number of owner-occupied households still increases by 7.2 percent. In fact, it is hard to generate within this model a truly pessimistic scenario for the nation as a whole, given the almost certain increase in the size of the population and the number of people in the forty-five–sixty-four age bracket.

Caveats

The simplicity of the model and the assumptions regarding the likely changes in the exogenous variables require the attachment of a number of caveats to the forecasts. One that is particularly apparent is the aggregate nature of the model. There will certainly be variation in the outcomes among the many groups that comprise the aggregate value of the owner-occupied housing stock. One group especially relevant to the topic of this book is the value of the housing stock within central cities. Surely, some cities will do better than the average and others will do worse; however, consideration of recent trends among some cities and aspects of central city housing markets suggest that many large cities are more likely to experience outcomes below the average.

Consider, first, how the parameterization of the model may differ for a large central city relative to other geographic areas. The principal difference is that the elasticity of supply is lower in the city because of the limited availability of land, tougher zoning restrictions, the dominance of the existing stock, and other competing uses of land, e.g., commercial real estate. All else being equal, a lower supply elasticity moves us in the direction of the Mankiw-Weil results if evidence of declines in demand can be found.

Second, consider likely changes in the principal exogenous variables in the system: population and income. Long-term trends in the United States and other countries indicate that populations have become increasingly decentralized and, as a result, city populations comprise a smaller and smaller fraction of the total population. In some large cities, the absolute population has decreased substantially, too, e.g., St. Louis, Detroit.

A story can be told that suggests income growth in the cities will also be less than that for the rest of the economy. Evidence exists to show that higher-income households are more likely to depart the central cities than low- and moderate-income households, so even if the incomes of low-income households increased at the same rate as other groups, growth among city residents may actually decline. Furthermore, a debate is underway that explores changes in the income distribution. Evidence appears to be mounting that the incomes at the bottom part of the distribution are increasing less rapidly, and even declining, relative to other parts of the distribution. (See, for example, Duncan, Rodgers, and Smeeding 1991.)

One can concoct a rather dismal forecast based upon these considerations. Cities that experience absolute population and income declines will, as a result, see a decline in the demand for housing. Furthermore, such a decline may have a substantial negative impact upon the asset price of existing housing because the supply is more likely to be inelastic. In a normal and efficiently operating housing market, such a decline in the asset price may serve as an incentive for households to return to the city to obtain housing at "bargain" prices. Unfortunately, experiences of the past few decades show that reversals in the flight to the suburbs are the exceptions to the rule, not the dominant pattern.

This pessimistic scenario ought to be considered something that might happen, not something that I forecast to occur on a large scale. The success or failure of the housing markets of the central city economies are dependent upon many more considerations than are contained in the simple model of the housing market outlined in this chapter. Nonetheless, I do believe that the cities are probably more at risk than most other segments of the economy absent major improvements in the public's view of the quality of life within many of our central cities.

Rental Real Estate

Although the focus of this chapter is owner-occupied housing, a few comments are in order regarding private rental real estate. The dominant components of rental real estate include rental housing and office buildings. The comments draw heavily upon two recent papers on which I have collaborated, Follain, Leavens, and Velz (1992) and Follain, Hendershott, and Ling (1992), as well as recent work by Hendershott and Kane (1992).

Rental Housing

The model of the rental housing market is quite similar to that for the owner-occupied market. One principal difference is the effect of tax policy upon the cost of rental compared with owner-occupied housing. Rental housing is a depreciable asset for tax purposes, and the rent at which such housing is offered in the marketplace to tenants is influenced by tax policy regarding depreciation. Rental housing is also much more affected by vacancy considerations than the owner-occupied housing market because of the higher mobility among renters compared with owners. Other differences can also be identified, but for the most part the model, its parameterization, and its forecasts of the relevant exogenous variables are similar for both renter and owner-occupied housing.

The rental housing market has been quite volatile in the 1980s, as has tax policy toward it. The Economic Recovery and Tax Act of 1981 (ERTA) conveyed substantial tax benefits to rental housing, but the 1986 Tax Reform Act (TRA) took them away. The experience of the 1980s was also influenced by the excessive real estate lending provided during the S&L debacle. The rental housing market during the 1980s reflected these changes. After rising during the early and mid-1980s, real rents and multifamily construction finally began to level off and even decline in the late 1980s and early 1990s. The number of renter households also increased in absolute numbers and as a percent of all households. Vacancy rates are higher than at the beginning of the 1980s but down from their peaks in the latter part of the 1980s.

My own sense is that the rental housing market will continue its return to normal. This is not necessarily good news for renters because returning to normal implies that vacancy rates will decline and the full effect of TRA will take hold during the 1990s. In particular, a return to normal probably implies a 10 percent or more increase in real rents during the 1990s. Although this will be good news for investors in rental housing and builders of rental housing, such an increase may cause additional hardship among renter households, especially those in the low end of the income distribution.

Office Space

Economists have only recently begun to focus on the behavioral relationships underlying the market for nonresidential real estate office space, so it is not possible to specify with much precision the various equations that are needed to forecast the market for nonresidential real estate in the 1990s. It is certainly true that the demand for such real estate stems from the use of real estate in the production of some other final product. Thus, the demand for office space is a derived demand that depends, ultimately, upon the demand for the final good being produced and the role of real estate in the production of that good. Unfortunately, economists know precious little about the role of real estate in the production process.

Hendershott and Kane offer an excellent overview of the trends in these markets during the past twenty years or so. They present evidence that suggests that the 1970s were a prototypical real estate cycle: overbuilding in the early 1970s led to a severe cutback of new construction and decreases in vacancy rates. The stage was set for another boom in the early 1980s because office vacancy rates had fallen below 4 percent. Indeed, a boom occurred that lasted well into the mid-1980s. Besides the pressures stemming from low vacancy rates, stimuli for the enormous nonresidential construction boom were provided for by ERTA and the excessive lending associated with the S&L debacle.

Hendershott and Kane argue that the consequences of the nonresidential boom of the 1980s remain. Vacancy rates are still high, and market rents for office space have continued to decline in several markets. Declines in the values of much nonresidential real estate have occurred, and more losses will probably be realized before the market returns to anything near equilibrium. My own sense, which is consistent with the analysis of Hendershott and Kane, is that the 1990s will be a period of continued adjustment for this market. Perhaps some semblance of normality will return by the year 2000, but it seems very unlikely that another boom in either construction or nonresidential property values is on the horizon for most areas of the country. What is probably more likely in the near term is a series of new announcements of real estate deals gone sour, e.g., Olympia and York.

Summary and Policy Forecast

Forecasts of the state of our world in the year 2000 have probably been made since the year 1001. They share some common traits: The forecasters are bold; few will examine whether the forecasts prove accurate; and most forecasts are predicated upon a host of assumptions, beliefs, and calculations that are difficult to justify to everyone's satisfaction. The fact that 2000 is only seven years away makes my forecasting job easier than the ones attempted in 1001, but the same traits apply.

Nonetheless and for the reasons offered above, I believe the following: The value of the owner-occupied housing stock will continue to improve in the next ten years or so. A real increase in excess of 25 percent is possible and, indeed, likely. A primary impetus for this growth is the belief that income and population will continue to grow in the 1990s. If this belief proves to be incorrect and the user cost of owner-occupied housing increases in the 1990s, then a decline is possible. However, even the worst-case scenario depicted in this chapter for the asset price of the typical owner-occupied house falls well short of the rather dire predictions made by some other economists.

Of course, a competitive, market-oriented economy will generate much variation around this mean prediction. One group that receives special attention in this chapter is the owner-occupied housing stock of some large central cities in which population and income declines are possible and, perhaps, likely. Such declines in combination with a relatively inelastic supply of housing may generate large declines in the demand for owner-occupied housing within some cities, although forecasts for specific cities are not offered. In an ideal, competitive, and market-oriented economy, such declines would be expected to generate substantial movement to the central city in order to take advantage of the lower-priced housing in the cities. Unfortunately, recent experience suggests that a return to the city is unlikely in many large cities given the broadly held perceptions about the quality of life within these cities.

Let me conclude with one final and more qualitatively oriented forecast regarding public policy toward owner-occupied housing in the 1990s. I believe that the pressure to reduce the subsidy to high-income homeowners will increase substantially in the 1990s. The subsidy to which I refer is the one implicit in our federal income tax system that exempts in-kind rental income from owner-occupied housing from taxable income yet permits the deduction of mortgage interest. The qualifier, "high-income," must be emphasized in this prediction because the support for a subsidy to support homeownership among low- and middle-income households is as strong as ever and justifiable, in my opinion. Furthermore, along with David Ling (1991), I argue that the tax subsidy to many middle-income homeowners has already been reduced substantially because of the Tax Reform Act of 1986 and see no reason why a further and direct assault on the subsidy to this portion of the income distribution is appropriate.

What is more difficult to justify is the large absolute and relative amount of the subsidy directed to high-income households. According to our calculations (Follain and Ling 1991), the tax subsidy to homeowners in 1989 exceeded $80 billion. Furthermore, the bulk of the subsidy is distributed to high-income households; 30 percent goes to those with adjusted gross incomes in excess of $75,000 and 55 percent to those with incomes in excess of $50,000. Surely, these subsidies ought to be examined carefully if, as I suspect, efforts are increased to reduce the federal deficit during the 1990s.

Notes

1. An estimate of the value of the stock exclusive of land is provided in Musgrave (1992), 106–37, Tables 10 and 12. The value of the housing stock inclusive of land is, roughly, the product of the average price of existing units (about $90,000) and the number of owner-occupied housing units (about sixty million), or about $5.4 trillion.
2. Several largely technical articles have been written in the past year or so that take issue with the Mankiw-Weil results. For example, see several papers in *Regional Science and Urban Economics*, Volume 21 (1991), and Swan 1992.

3. A survey of much of the evidence on estimates of the income and price elasticities of the demand for housing can be found in Mayo 1981.

4. The series in Figure 4.3 is based upon the characteristics of a new single-family house constructed in 1987, which is the most recent index available from the Bureau of the Census in its *Construction Report C–27.*

5. Surveys and discussions of some of the evidence can be found in Olsen 1987, and Stover 1986.

6. The aggregate homeownership rate masks the actual declines in homeownership in the United States. In fact, the homeownership rates among married couples of all age groups declined substantially during the 1980s. The aggregate rate did not move down as much because the age distribution of the population moved toward those groups with higher than average homeownership rates. This point is made by Haurin, Hendershott, and Ling 1988.

7. An excellent collection of work in this area and useful surveys can be found in a special issue of *Housing Finance Review,* edited by Patric Hendershott, Summer 1989.

8. I calculate this elasticity in a very simple way. The percentage change in the number of homeowners generated by a change in the age distribution of the population can be written as:

$$\frac{\partial HO}{\partial n_i} \frac{n_i}{HO} = (h_i ho_i - h_j ho_j) \frac{n_i POP}{HO}$$

The homeownership rate for the forty-five–sixty-four age group is about .72 percent and the homeownership rate for the other age groups is about .62 percent. Assume the average household size is about 2.67 persons for both groups and the headship rate is $\frac{1}{2.67}$. Then the percentage change in the *HO* for a 1 percent change in n_i evaluated at $n_i = .3$ and $POP = 250$ million is about .33.

9. Mankiw and Weil (1989) would agree that in the very long run the asset price would revert to replacement cost, except, perhaps, for some land price effects.

10. See Poterba (1991), who suggests that this may occur during the 1990s if households are slow to adjust their inflationary expectations. He posits that households were reluctant to reduce their expectations based upon the 1970s to the realities of the 1980s. If households are generally slow to adjust and focus upon recent experiences, then they may lower their expectations during the 1990s. All else being equal, lower expectations of housing prices increase the user cost of owner-occupied housing.

11. Follain and Ling (1991), discuss this point. They show that the combination of a higher standard deduction and reduced opportunities for nonhousing expense deductions reduce the value of the mortgage interest deduction for many middle-income households. This reduced value will, in turn, increase the user cost of owner-occupied housing.

References

Duncan, Greg; Rodgers, William; and Smeeding, Timothy S. 1991. "Why Is the Middle-Class Shrinking?" Metropolitan Studies Working Paper, Syracuse University.

Fair, Ray C., and Dominguez, Kathryn M. 1991. "Effects of the Changing U.S. Age Distribution on Macroeconomic Equations." *American Economic Review* (December): 1276–94.

Federal Reserve System. 1991. *Balance Sheets for the U.S. Economy 1945–1990*. Washington, D.C.: Board of Governors.

Follain, James R.; Hendershott, Patric H.; and Ling, David C. 1987. "Understanding the Real Estate Provisions of Tax Reform: Motivation and Impact." *National Tax Journal* (September): 363–72.

———. 1992. "Real Estate Markets Since 1980: What Role Have Tax Changes Played?" *National Tax Journal* (September): 253–66.

Follain, James R.; Leavens, Donald; and Velz, Orawin. 1992. "Identifying the Effects of Tax Reform on Multifamily Rental Housing." *Journal of Urban Economics* (May): 337–59.

Follain, James R., and Ling, David C. 1991. "The Federal Tax Subsidy to Housing and the Reduced Value of the Mortgage Interest Deduction." *National Tax Journal* (June): 147–68.

Haurin, Don; Hendershott, Patric H.; and Ling, David C. 1988. "Home Ownership Rates of Married Couples: An Econometric Investigation." *Housing Finance Review* 7 (Summer): 85–108.

Hendershott, Patric H., and Kane, Edward J. 1992. "Causes and Consequences of the 1980s Construction Boom." *Journal of Applied Corporate Finance* (May): 61–70.

Ling, David C. Forthcoming. "The Price of Owner-Occupied Housing Services: 1973–1989." In Sa-Aadu, ed., *Research in Real Estate,* Volume 4.

Mankiw, N. Gregory, and Weil, David N. 1989. "The Baby Boom, the Baby Bust, and the Housing Market." *Regional Science and Urban Economics* 19: 235–55.

Mayo, S.K. 1981. "Theory and Estimation in the Economics of Housing Demand." *Journal of Urban Economics* 10: 338–56.

Mills, Edwin S., ed. 1987. *Handbook of Regional and Urban Economics,* Volume 2. New York: N.Y.: Elsevier Science Publishing Company, Inc.

Musgrave, John. 1992. "Fixed Reproducible Tangible Wealth in the United States, Revised Estimates." *Survey of Current Business* (January): 106–37.

Olsen, Edgar O. 1987. "The Demand and Supply of Housing Service: A Critical Survey of the Empirical Literature." In Mills, ed., *Handbook of Regional and Urban Economics,* Volume 2, chapter 25.

Peters, Donald L. 1988. "Receipts and Expenditures of State Governments and of Local Governments, Revised and Updated Estimates, 1984–1987." *Survey of Current Business* (September): 23–5.

Poterba, James. 1991. "House Price Dynamics: The Role of Tax Policy and Demography." *Brookings Papers on Economic Activity* 2: 143–83.

Sa-Aadu, Jarjisu, ed. Forthcoming. *Research in Real Estate,* Volume 4.

Stover, Mark Edward. 1986. "The Price Elasticity of the Supply of Single-Family Detached Housing." *Journal of Urban Economics* 20: 331–40.

Swan, Craig. 1992. "The Demand for Housing and House Prices." Unpublished manuscript, University of Minnesota.

U.S. Bureau of the Census, *Statistical Abstract of the U.S.:* 1991, (111th edition).

5

Are City Fiscal Crises on the Horizon?

ANDREW RESCHOVSKY

Introduction

In many parts of the country the beginning of the 1990s has been a period of often dramatic declines in the value of real estate. For example:

- In Boston, condominiums that were worth $250,000 in 1988 were selling for under $150,000 in early 1992.
- Again in Boston, office towers have fallen dramatically in value. Between 1988 and 1991 per-square-foot rents in some office buildings have fallen by as much as 50 percent. In 1992 the downtown office vacancy rate probably reached 20 percent, with a 50 percent vacancy rate in many new buildings.
- In New York City the market value of total taxable property fell by nearly 10 percent in 1990 and 1991.
- In Dallas, property values in 1992 were about 15 percent lower than they were in 1986.
- The market value of high-valued single-family homes in Los Angeles fell by over 11 percent in 1991.

These examples hide the fact that some property owners have been facing much larger than average declines in the value of their property. The savings and loan crisis has highlighted the fact that as the real estate market fell sharply in some areas, the owners of a substantial number of properties, especially commercial developments, defaulted on their mortgages, which in too many cases were held by (now-defunct) S&Ls. In addition, many homeowners are suffering from the decline in market values away from the glare of television cameras and out of sight of newspaper reporters. For example, in Boston, the value of many houses purchased in the late 1980s (1986-89) was 25 to 30 percent less in 1992 than the purchase price. The current value of many houses is below the amount of the outstanding mortgage. As a consequence, homeowners are, at best, locked into their current houses. Many of those who have lost their jobs will lose their homes and forfeit their downpayments.[1]

Although falling property values have a direct impact on individuals, the purpose of this chapter is to explore the impact of the decline in property values on big-city finances. Many big cities are in financial trouble; many face the near-term prospect of large budget deficits. Discussions of large service cuts, increases in city taxes and fees, and in a few cases the possibility of bankruptcy are regularly reported in the press. Crystal-ball gazing is a risky business, and I don't claim any special proficiency. In fact, I must admit, that as I have been thinking about this question, my crystal ball has become cloudier. Nevertheless, I would like to speculate about whether the ongoing decline in property tax bases will lead to a rash of city fiscal crises, with city governments unable to function in an ordinary manner.

A second purpose of this chapter is to explore the options available to city governments facing serious fiscal problems induced by falling property values or other factors.

I have found it useful to address the question of whether declines in market value will result in fiscal crisis in large American cities by asking five specific questions:

• *How important is the property tax in the financing of city services?* As the most direct link between market values and the fiscal health of cities is the property tax, we must begin by asking what role the property tax plays in financing city governments.

• *Are the current declines in market values an ordinary cyclical occurrence?* Are declines in property values common events in large cities, occurring with some regularity during recessions? Are property values naturally cyclical, and are we now observing the down side of a boom-and-bust pattern that has been repeated often in history? Or are there indications that the pattern we are currently observing is somehow unique?

• *Can we expect market values to rebound quickly and to continue growing at a reasonable rate?* Even if market values are depressed now, can we expect them to rebound quickly?

• *Have falling property values been reflected in shrinking city tax bases?* As the property tax is levied on the assessed value of properties, we must ask how well changes in the real estate market are reflected in city tax bases, namely, the assessed value of property. This is a question about both the efficiency of tax administration and about fiscal institutions put in place explicitly to loosen the link between the real estate market and a city's property tax base.

• *How do we recognize a city fiscal crisis?* What questions should we ask? Will shrinking property tax bases lead to municipal bankruptcies? What difficulties will cities face in providing "reasonable" levels of public services at affordable rates of taxation?

Measuring changes in the market of real property in American cities is not an easy task. There exist no comprehensive national data on trends in the market value of property. The most recent data for a broad sample of U.S. cities date from 1981.[2] The only way to compile current data on market values is to collect them on a city-by-city basis; I have, therefore, chosen to concentrate my attention on the experiences of a handful of large cities that have experienced large recent reductions in property values. Although these cities do not constitute in any way a random sample of all large cities, I believe their experiences in the last few years are indicative of broader trends as well as being of interest in their own right.[3]

How Important Is the Property Tax
in the Financing of City Services?

As documented by Dick Netzer in chapter 3, over the course of this century the property tax has been slowly declining as a source of municipal finance. Nevertheless, in many large cities, it still accounts for an important portion of locally raised revenues. The property tax accounted for nearly 29 percent of own-source general revenue and 42.5 percent of own-source tax revenue in FY 1989 in the nation's fifty-three largest cities. This percentage understates the impact of the property tax on residents of big cities because forty-five of the largest fifty-three cities have independent school districts that rely on it heavily.

The importance of the property tax varies substantially among cities currently experiencing declining property values. On one extreme, Boston gets about 64 percent of its total locally raised revenue from the property tax. On the other extreme, Philadelphia relies on the property tax for less than 15 percent of its total own-source revenue. In between are Los Angeles (20 percent), New York City (32 percent), Dallas (37 percent), and Baltimore (52 percent).

To the extent that weak real estate markets do in fact translate into reductions in property tax revenues, nearly all cities will be affected, but clearly the potential impact of falling property values will be greater in cities like Boston that rely heavily on the property tax.

Are the Current Declines in Market Values
an Ordinary Cyclical Occurrence?

Data series on changes in the market value of property in the nation's largest cities are simply not available. Thus, it is not possible to provide a definitive answer to a question about the cyclical nature of property values. Although the current recession has almost certainly had a negative impact on property values, it appears that those cities where property values have fallen the most are those cities that experienced the largest increases in property values during the 1980s. Based on limited data, it also appears that while during recent recessions market values may have stagnated, actual declines in value were relatively rare. In California, for example, housing prices rose rapidly from the mid-1970s through 1981; despite the severe recession during the early 1980s, housing prices in California stopped increasing but did not decline. As the housing market softens, homeowners tend to respond by staying put or by leaving homes on the market for a long period, until they get an offer at or near the asking price. In a recent paper, Karl Case and Robert Shiller (1988) drew on a survey of recent homebuyers to explore the reasons that residential real estate prices tend to be sticky downward. Among the reasons they suggest for observed price rigidity are the high transactions cost involved in selling a house, a psychological disposition to hold on to losing investments so as "to avoid the pain of regret," and a widely held belief that waiting may in fact pay off.

Although the statistical evidence is limited, it appears that the current decline in market values, especially in the residential real estate market, is a relatively rare phenomenon, one that is not automatically associated with economic downturns.

Can We Expect Market Values to Rebound Quickly and to Continue Growing at a Reasonable Rate?

There is no easy answer to this question. As James Follain indicates in chapter 4, there is considerable debate over the future of housing prices. In a study that has received a great deal of attention, Mankiw and Weil (1989) predicted a fall in the real price of housing of nearly 50 percent over the next twenty years. Follain, on the other hand, argues that the real value of housing will increase modestly during the 1990s. If a city's underlying economy remains strong, there are good reasons to believe market values will rebound. One hypothesis is that in cities such as Houston and Dallas, which had market values that were near the national average before values started to decline, we can expect a complete and relatively rapid rebound of prices. In the Northeast and in California, it is reasonable to assume that speculative pressures pushed housing values much higher than the national average and that now that the speculative bubble has burst, real estate prices will take many years to return to their previous (nominal) highs. Karl Case (1991) suggests that in Boston, following a tremendous boom and a precipitous decline, the real estate market has returned to about where it was in 1984. He points out, however, that in 1984 the Massachusetts economy was much stronger than it is now. In 1984 the state unemployment rate was 4.8 percent, while in early 1992 it was over 9.1 percent. This suggests, that at least in Boston, recovery of the real estate market will take a long time.

It is also likely that the market value of central city office buildings will experience limited growth well into the 1990s. Vacancy rates in major downtown office buildings have been increasing over the past several years (CB Commercial 1991). Although in many of the nation's largest cities on the east and west coasts, vacancy rates are still below the national average (as of December 1991), several factors suggest that rates may rise in 1993 and beyond, continuing to put downward pressure on the market values of commercial property. In a number of cities, large office building projects that were begun in 1988 and 1989 are just now coming onto the market, further increasing the excess supply of office space. In addition, mortgages on a number of downtown commercial buildings (especially second tier, class B property) were held by now bankrupt savings and loans. Many of these properties are now held by the Federal Deposit Insurance Company or the Resolution Trust Corporation. Both of these organizations have strong incentives to sell these properties as quickly as possible, further depressing the commercial real estate market.

Have Falling Property Values Been Reflected in Shrinking City Tax Bases?

A weak real estate market will have a direct impact on a city's property tax base only if the *assessed value* of property is reduced to reflect falling market values. Until quite recently, in most cities changes in assessments were made infrequently. In some cases, decades passed between reassessments (Oldman and Aaron 1965). As long as reassessments were conducted infrequently, taxpayers were unaffected by either increases or decreases in the market value of their property. However, a direct consequence of infrequent assessments was a high degree of assessment inequity between and within neighborhoods.

Two things happened about fifteen years ago that led to substantial improvements in the quality of assessments in many parts of the country. First was the widespread adoption of Computer Assisted Mass Assessment (CAMA) techniques. CAMA relies on the development of a hedonic index based on data on the physical and locational characteristics of a sample of recently sold properties. Assessed values for properties that have not sold are determined by values attributed to each characteristic from the hedonic regression. The major impact of CAMA is that it allows local governments to completely reassess all property on an annual or biannual basis.

A series of state court decisions, for the most part in the late 1970s, also led to greatly improved assessment quality. In a number of states, including New York, Texas, and Massachusetts, the courts ruled that assessments had to be conducted in a timely fashion and had to reflect the true market value of property.

As a result of these two factors, falling market values in a number of states are probably for the first time being quite accurately reflected in assessed values. Let me provide two examples: In Boston, the assessed value of property mirrored the rapid rise in market values during most of the 1980s and the steep decline during the beginning of the 1990s. Because by statute assessed values in any given fiscal year reflect the market values six months before the start of the fiscal year, the downturn in assessments lags the downturn in the real estate market. Thus, the assessed value of all taxable property reached a peak of $36.4 billion in FY 1991 and then fell by 18 percent to $29.8 billion in FY 1992 (City of Boston 1991). Although the housing market bottomed out by the third quarter of 1991, it appears that the value of commercial property, especially in the Boston Central Business District, is continuing to fall (during the first half of 1992). Thus, it is extremely likely that the value of Boston's tax base will be lower in FY 1993 than in FY 1992.

Texas has experienced a severe and more protracted decline in property values than most of the rest of the country. The precipitous drop in petroleum prices in the mid-1980s led to a decline in the value of property starting in 1985. In Houston, the market hit bottom in FY 1989, while in Dallas prices were falling through FY 1991. In both cities the assessed value of property has followed the decline of market values quite closely (State of Texas 1992).

Another important reason that assessed values tend to reflect falling market values is that owners of property, especially commercial property, are highly motivated to appeal their assessments (apply for an abatement). In recent years there has been a growth of firms, sometimes franchised, that will file commercial appeals on a contingency basis. The major bond-rating agencies have recently paid increased attention to the magnitude of cities' "abatement liabilities." City governments must convince the rating agencies that they are not going to have to abate large amounts of property tax revenue as a result of successful appeals of assessments. This implicit pressure from the bond-rating agencies is likely to lead to relatively conservative assessments of commercial property.

In a falling real estate market, homeowners, especially those anxious to sell, are more likely to appeal their assessments because they are too low rather than too high. Especially in cities with large amounts of nonresidential property, these appeals by homeowners are likely to be unsuccessful because the consequence of overassessing residential property is that city residents will collectively have to bear a larger share of the city's property tax levy relative to the owners of business property.

Prior to the series of court cases mandating full market value assessments, residential property tended to be assessed at a much lower proportion of market value than commercial and industrial property. The process of bringing all property up to its market value would have resulted in a substantial shift in the total property tax levy from business to residential taxpayers. The potential political consequences of increased property taxes on residents, with no corresponding increase in public services, led a number of states to search for ways to prevent this shift. Several states, including Massachusetts, adopted a system of property tax classi fication that allowed local governments to tax residential property at a lower rate than nonresidential property. In California in 1978, the voters approved Proposition 13, which not only placed a 1 percent ceiling on effective property tax rates but limited increases in the assessed value of individual properties to 2 percent per annum, unless the property was sold, in which case its assessment would be increased to reflect its current market value.

An important (perhaps unintended) consequence of Proposition 13 is that local governments are partially sheltered from the consequences of declining market values. For example, in San Francisco, where market values grew rapidly in the late 1980s, property tax revenues actually increased by an annual rate of about 10 percent even though the property tax rate was slightly reduced. The rapid growth in property taxes occurred because of a quite active real estate market, allowing in many cases dramatic increases in the assessed value of the properties being sold. Since 1990, although property values in San Francisco have been falling, total assessed value continues to rise, albeit at a much slower annual rate (about 5 percent). To see how rising assessed values can occur as market values fall, consider a house, assessed at $75,000, that has been lived in by the same owner since the early 1970s. In 1990 assume that this house had a market value of $400,000. Since then, its value has fallen by 12.5 percent to $350,000, at which price it is sold. Although its value has fallen in recent years, its assessed value suddenly climbs by $275,000.

New York State responded to a court case (*Hellerstein v. Assessor, Town of Islip*) that would have resulted in a substantial shift of property tax liabilities from commercial-industrial to residential taxpayers, by allowing local governments to tax residential property at a different rate from nonresidential property. In addition, the state passed a law requiring that any assessment increases on most types of property had to be phased in over a period of several years. Thus, for example, for one-, two-, or three-family houses, assessment increases cannot exceed 6 percent in any given year or 20 percent over a five-year period. Annual assessment increases on large apartment buildings (over ten units) and on commercial-industrial property are not limited but must be phased in over five years. The consequence of these assessment limits is that while market values in New York City have fallen by about 10 percent over the past three years, total assessed value has continued to climb—by about 9 percent per year between 1989 and 1991 and by 3 percent from 1991 to 1992 (City of New York 1992).

New York's assessment restrictions shelter taxpayers from rapid increases in assessed value. As a consequence, the city's tax base only partially reflected the explosive growth in market values that occurred during the 1980s. The flip side of this is that when property values began to fall, the city's tax base continued to rise. New York City is currently projecting rates of growth in its tax base of about 1 percent per year for FY 1993 and FY 1994 (New York State Financial Control Board 1991). As New York City currently is facing a deficit, the fact that its property tax base is stable in light of a declining real estate market is a big plus.

Despite the fact that the quality of assessments is quite high in many cities, assessors, who tend to be conservative, often set assessed values a little below market values. This means that we should not expect modest declines in market value to be reflected in falling assessed values. As noted above, a number of states have taken steps to insulate taxpayers from the impact of increasing assessments. From the standpoint of municipal finance, these actions reduce the ability of local governments to tap the expansion in the real wealth of its citizens. At the same time these provisions tend to protect governments from one direct consequence of economic downturns, namely, a reduction in the size of the property tax base.

How Do We Recognize a City Fiscal Crisis?

In order to predict the likely impact of declining property values on the fiscal health of big cities, it is important to start with a clear picture of cities' current fiscal health. If one relies on reports in the press, it is clear that big cities are in very bad fiscal condition. Let's review some of the recent reports: In the spring of 1991 Philadelphia was on the verge of bankruptcy, facing a FY 1992 deficit of $230 million and the adamant refusal of the banking community to lend it any more money. Only by agreeing to accept the control of a fiscal watchdog agency appointed by the state, did Philadelphia regain limited access to the credit markets. In 1991 New York City faced the prospect of a $3.3 billion deficit for FY 1992. Only by raising property tax rates and instituting major spending cuts will the city be able to balance its budget. San Francisco is also in the throes of a fiscal crisis: Current projections indicate a FY 1993 general fund deficit of $120 million (out of a $1.5 billion budget). The city's new mayor campaigned on a pledge not to raise taxes, a pledge he continues to support. At the same time he continues to promise that there will be no service cuts. The outcome is unclear.

Despite the dramatic nature of these stories, they fail to provide an accurate picture of the fiscal position of city governments. They reflect budgetary practices and the consequences of short-term events. To get a good sense of the ''structural'' fiscal health of a city government requires knowledge of how well the city government performs its basic function, the provision of public services to city residents, *relative* to the burden it places on its residents. Thus a city that always balances its budget and provides a minimum level of public services may be in very weak fiscal health if it must tax residents at extraordinarily high rates. Alternatively, a city that manages to maintain both balanced budgets and moderate tax rates may nevertheless be fiscally stressed if its level of service provision is very low, with, for example, trash infrequently collected, police not available, and large classes in its schools. The fact that a city goes bankrupt or doesn't go bankrupt is not necessarily a good indicator of its fiscal health.[4]

I want to argue that it is most useful to focus on the *structural* components of a city's fiscal health, rather than on its short-run budgetary situation. Following Bradbury et al. (1984), let me define a city's fiscal condition as a gap, expressed in dollars per capita, between a city's *expenditure need* and *revenue-raising capacity*. A city's expenditure need indicates the amount that it must spend per resident to provide an average level of public services given its service responsibilities and the harshness of its environment for providing services. A harsh environment increases the costs of providing services, where costs reflect the effects of city characteristics that are outside the control of city officials. A city's revenue-raising capacity indicates the amount of revenue per resident it has available if residents of all cities face the same tax burden.

If this gap, called the *need-capacity gap* is large, a city government will be forced to provide less-than-average-quality public services and/or burden its residents with higher-than-average taxes. Cities in weak fiscal condition by this measure will find it particularly hard to compete with surrounding suburban communities for middle- and high-income residents and for jobs for its residents.

In their book *America's Ailing Cities,* Helen Ladd and John Yinger (1991) provide a measure of the fiscal health of the nation's largest cities using a variant of the need-capacity gap. They find that many of the nation's largest central cities are in very weak fiscal health, with expenditure need substantially greater than revenue-raising capacity. Based on data for 1982, they conclude that the fourteen central cities in the weakest fiscal health would on average have to raise their revenue-raising capacity by 13 percent in order to provide their residents with an average quality of public services while imposing an average tax burden on them. Among the cities in the weakest fiscal position are New York City, New Orleans, and Detroit. Cities in weak fiscal health generally face a number of structural fiscal problems: first, they operate in a harsh fiscal environment, where the costs of providing services are high; second, they often have a wide range of service responsibilities mandated by higher levels of government or by the courts; and third, they face substantial loss in their economic base, as measured in part by falling city employment, especially in the high-wage manufacturing sector.

Ladd and Yinger (1991) demonstrate that the growth in the economy during the 1980s increased the revenue-raising capacity of many large cities. However, the resulting improvements in the fiscal conditions of city governments were offset by two important trends. First, in almost all cities a series of developments over the past decade, most notably the crack-cocaine epidemic, the spread of AIDS, and the explosion of homelessness, have made the fiscal environment much harsher. Although no precise data are available, these factors have undoubtedly raised the costs of public services and increased the expenditure need of many, if not all, large cities. Second, during the past decade cities have had to become steadily more self reliant. During this period the amount of federal aid received by city governments has been dramatically reduced. In Boston, the proportion of general revenue coming from federal grants fell by more than half between 1979 and 1989, from 9 percent to under 4 percent. In San Francisco, the federal share of general revenue fell from 14 to 5 percent during the same ten-year period (U.S. Bureau of the Census 1991). Similar reductions occurred in most large cities.

City governments have been further buffeted by state cuts in grants-in-aid. Gold (1992) reports that in 1991 fourteen states reduced their general assistance to local governments. In some states aid cuts have been substantial. For example, state general-purpose aid to Boston has been cut by about $80 million between FY 1989 and FY 1992 and will be level funded in FY 1993. This amounts to a constant-dollar reduction in aid of 32 percent.

To date no data are available to indicate whether recent state aid cutbacks have favored suburban and rural communities at the expense of large urban communities. However, it appears that a politically popular way of cutting aid is to reduce each community's aid by an equal percentage. When the initial distribution of aid favors big cities, the result of equal percentage cuts is a larger reduction in aid relative to total spending in big cities than in smaller places.[5]

The fiscal health of city governments may also be hurt by state government cuts in social service expenditures. A growing number of states are substantially reducing welfare programs, in particular general assistance. Cuts in Medicaid coverage are also widespread. As many of the beneficiaries of these programs are big-city residents, it is at least possible, and I suspect probable, that an unintended effect of these state budget cuts will be increased costs for city governments. This shifting of costs from state to local governments may occur if people whose state-funded benefits are cut end up in cities' homeless shelters, in the emergency rooms of city hospitals, or in cities' criminal justice systems.

At the beginning of this chapter I posed the following question: Will the decline in property values in many of the nation's large cities lead to a new round of fiscal crises? The answer, I believe is that although a shrinking tax base will complicate the fiscal problems faced by city governments, its impact on the structural fiscal problems of cities will be relatively minor. The combination of rising costs, declining federal, and in some cases state, fiscal assistance, and deteriorating economic conditions in many of the nation's largest cities suggests that the fiscal condition of these cities is deteriorating. A temporary fall in market values will certainly exacerbate the fiscal situation, but by itself will not create a new wave of budgetary crises.

Most of the cities experiencing the largest reductions in property values also benefited from the largest increases in values during the late 1980s. I would contend that for many of these cities, the rapid run-up in prices had the effect of delaying the most visible signs of the underlying fiscal crisis. The current fall in market values works in the other direction.

How Can Cities Respond to Falling Market Values?

In the rest of the chapter I turn to the question of how cities can respond to falling market values. My primary focus will be on the option of increasing property tax rates. I will also briefly consider two other options: cutting public spending and adopting alternative revenue sources.

Increasing Property Tax Rates

Raising nominal property tax rates seems like the obvious response to reduced assessed values. Unless rates are raised, nominal property tax liabilities will actually decline for property owners whose property has lost value. Since property taxes are paid out of current income and even during a recession income remains constant or increases for most taxpayers, increases in rates won't increase burdens as long as total property tax liabilities increase less rapidly than incomes.

The argument for raising nominal property tax rates is strengthened by the fact that in a substantial number of large cities, property tax burdens declined during much of the 1980s.[6] For examples, consider the recent fiscal history in Boston, New York, and San Francisco:

Boston. In 1980 Massachusetts adopted a property tax classification system that allowed local governments to tax residential property at a substantially lower rate than commercial-industrial property. In 1981, with the passage of Proposition 2½, effective property tax rates were limited to 2½ percent, and annual property tax increases were limited to 2½ percent of the current levy, plus the tax levied on new construction. As a consequence of classification and Proposition 2½, and a very strong construction boom during the mid-1980s, Boston was able to reduce residential property taxes over the past decade. In current dollars, the average tax on single-family homes and condominiums declined from $1,732 in FY 1981 to $1,211 in FY 1992 (City of Boston 1991). In constant dollars this represents a tax reduction of 60 percent. Measured relative to income, the average residential property tax burden declined from 4.1 percent in FY 1981 to 1.9 percent in FY 1992.

New York City. Owners of single and duplex houses are favored by the property tax system in New York. During the 1980s, the tax burden shifted increasingly away from those residents and toward owners of apartment buildings and commercial property. Although tax levies on one- and two-family houses rose in nominal terms during the 1980s, the rate of increase was below the rate of inflation. In the ten years since 1979 the market value of residential property increased dramatically. As a result, the effective residential property tax rate fell by more than half, from 2.15 percent in 1979 to 0.85 percent in 1989 (Chernick 1992).

San Francisco. Because of Proposition 13, effective property tax rates depend primarily on the length of time since properties were last sold. In the active and rapidly rising San Francisco real estate market during the latter half of the 1980s, there was a sharp drop in the effective tax rates faced by property owners who chose not to move. Between 1981 and 1989 the nominal tax rate also fell, from 1.20 to 1.09 percent (City of San Francisco 1991).

Despite the fact that property tax burdens have declined in a number of cities during the 1980s, there is at least limited evidence that city governments are unwilling to raise rates even in the face of a shrinking tax base.

In California, where Proposition 13 has capped rates, raising rates is not an option, as cities already tax at the maximum 1 percent. In New York City, where property tax rates were raised in 1992, Mayor Dinkins promised not to raise rates for the next four years. In Boston, property tax rates have increased during the past three years from approximately $8 per thousand to $11 per thousand; however, the current rate is still only about half of the 1983 rate, and further rate increases are likely to be prevented by the 2½ percent levy limit mandated by Proposition 2½. Although Boston residents can vote to override the levy limit, the prospects of a successful override are small. Through FY 1990 none of the state's twenty-one city governments with populations over 50,000 had even attempted an override. In FY 1991, facing a falling real estate market and substantial cuts in state aid, five cities attempted an override, and only two were successful (Bradbury 1991).[7]

Why Property Tax Rates Won't Rise

Resistance to property tax rate increases is likely to continue not only in cities where property tax burdens have been rising, but also in cities like Boston and New York, where property tax burdens have been declining in recent years.

I believe there are two important reasons why city government officials are likely to oppose property tax rate increases. First is their desire to remain fiscally competitive with surrounding suburban communities. There is considerable evidence that tax rates and the quality of public services, especially schools, play a role in determining metropolitan area locational choices of both firms and individuals (Reschovsky 1979, Wasylenko 1980, McGuire 1985, Luce and Summers 1987). City officials recognize that regardless of whether their property tax rates are higher or lower than rates in surrounding communities, increases in city rates relative to suburban rates will lead to outmigration by middle- and high-income residents and by business enterprises.[8]

Although comprehensive data are not available, it appears that in a number of metropolitan areas property values have fallen more in the central city than in many of the surrounding suburbs. For example, in Boston the average assessed value of existing property has fallen by about twice as much as property in the adjacent suburban communities. This pattern of changes in values obviously weakens the relative fiscal position of cities and implies that tax rate increases sufficient to maintain current property tax levies will result in an increase in the ratio of city to suburban tax rates. This puts cities in a difficult position. If they choose to maintain their relative tax rate vis-à-vis their suburbs, they will have to operate with reduced property tax revenues. On the other hand, if they raise their rates in order to increase or maintain property tax revenues, their competitive position is weakened.

A second, more speculative, reason city officials may resist any property tax rate increases involves the rising political costs of raising taxes. The newspapers are full of examples of voter anger at politicians who raise taxes or, in some cases, even propose to raise taxes. A prime example is New Jersey, where voters responded to a tax increase approved by a Democratic governor and legislature by providing the Republicans with a veto-proof majority in both houses of the legislature.

One explanation for this (presumed) rise in opposition to both increased public spending and taxes is that *distributional politics* has changed in the last decade or so. As demonstrated by the data in Table 5.1, cities have become more ethnically and racially heterogeneous. I hypothesize that as heterogeneity has increased, people have become much more conscious of the distribution of taxes and services among groups of city residents. I suspect that many people, especially in big cities, no longer assume that in return for paying their taxes, they get a bundle of services, such as police and fire protection, sanitation, and public education. Now the question that is asked is, "Will I benefit from a tax increase, or will it all go to 'them' [meaning peoples of other economic, social, or ethnic backgrounds]? If this question is in fact being asked, it means that, at least in the minds of many city residents, the link between taxes and benefits has been severed, or at best, weakened.

Those taxpayers for whom the link between changes in taxes and changes in benefits is broken may be much less willing to pay increased taxes to finance increased public spending. It is important to emphasize that changing attitudes and perceptions about public services do not necessarily tell us anything about the preferences for public services of the median voter, only that politically important subgroups of the population may have strongly divergent views.

In order to understand the impacts of these changing perceptions on governmental action it is important to have an underlying model of city government decision making. The conventional model focuses on the median or the "decisive" voter. It is as-

Table 5.1

Change in Minority Population between 1980 and 1990 in Thirty Largest American Cities

City	1990 Population (in percent)			Percentage Change from 1980*		
	Black	Asian	Hispanic	Black	Asian	Hispanic
New York	28.6	7.0	24.4	13.9	114.2	22.6
Los Angeles	14.0	9.8	39.9	−17.6	48.7	45.1
Chicago	39.1	3.7	19.6	−1.8	61.1	40.0
Houston	28.1	4.1	27.6	1.8	99.7	56.8
Philadelphia	39.9	2.7	5.6	5.6	157.5	47.4
San Diego	9.4	11.8	20.7	5.6	81.0	38.9
Detroit	75.7	0.8	2.8	20.0	49.0	16.7
Dallas	29.5	2.2	20.9	0.3	192.8	69.9
Phoenix	5.2	1.7	20.0	8.3	89.2	35.1
San Antonio	7.0	1.1	55.6	−4.1	74.7	3.5
San Jose	4.7	19.5	26.6	2.2	140.0	19.3
Baltimore	59.2	1.1	1.0	8.0	9.4	0.0
Indianapolis	22.6	0.9	1.1	3.7	67.8	22.2
San Francisco	10.9	29.1	13.9	−14.2	32.0	13.0
Jacksonville	25.2	1.9	2.6	−0.8	98.1	44.4
Columbus	22.6	2.4	1.1	2.3	188.5	37.5
Milwaukee	30.5	1.9	6.3	32.0	245.3	53.7
Memphis	54.8	0.8	0.7	15.1	92.8	−12.5
Washington, D.C.	65.8	1.8	5.4	−6.4	75.1	92.9
Boston	25.6	5.3	10.8	14.3	97.5	68.8
Seattle	10.1	11.8	3.6	6.3	59.5	38.5
El Paso	3.4	1.2	69.0	6.2	47.0	10.4
Cleveland	46.6	1.0	4.6	6.4	60.3	18.4
New Orleans	61.9	1.9	3.5	11.9	44.0	2.9
Nashville-Davidson	24.3	1.4	0.9	4.3	190.2	12.5
Denver	12.8	2.4	23.0	6.7	67.8	22.3
Austin	12.4	3.0	23.0	1.6	188.3	23.0
Fort Worth	22.0	2.0	19.5	−3.5	227.7	54.8
Oklahoma City	16.0	2.4	5.0	9.6	130.9	78.6
Portland, OR	7.7	5.3	3.2	1.3	86.3	52.4
Kansas City	29.6	1.2	3.9	8.0	60.0	18.2
Long Beach	13.7	13.6	23.6	21.2	154.9	68.6
St. Louis	47.5	0.9	1.3	4.2	148.6	8.3
Atlanta	67.1	0.9	1.9	0.8	80.0	35.7
Pittsburgh	25.8	1.6	0.9	7.5	161.9	12.5

Source: 1980 and 1990 U.S. Census, United States Summary, General Population Characteristic, Tables: Persons by Race and Sex for Areas and Places.
*Minus signs indicate the decrease in minority population from 1980 to 1990.

sumed that in order to get elected or reelected, politicians will support policies that reflect the preferences of the decisive voter. Building on the work of Inman (1989) and Chernick (1990), I would like to suggest a model of city government decision making that in contrast to the decisive-voter model, focuses on the impact of various *groups* of citizens within a city on the *political costs* of public decisions. Let us assume that politicians attempt to minimize a political cost function that includes a number of variables that reflect the distribution of public sector benefits and taxes within the city. From the perspective of the politician who must decide whether to propose increased taxes and spending, the political costs are likely to be lowest when politically powerful groups of voters perceive that they will receive net benefits from the proposed increases. On the other hand, political costs are likely to be highest when influential groups of voters believe that in relative terms, other groups of voters will receive the largest benefits. For example, a resident of a middle-class bedroom suburb is likely to believe that his children will benefit directly from a proposed increase in taxes used for public education, while a middle-class resident of a city may believe that extra tax revenue for education will primarily benefit other groups of children, such as those requiring special or remedial education. This implies that the political costs of proposing tax and spending increases may depend critically on the *distribution* of tax burdens and public spending benefits within a community.

The factors that affect the distribution of public service benefits within a community are thus likely to influence the political costs of decision making. For example, communities with a relatively large group of elderly residents may oppose tax increases, especially those for schools. The political costs of increasing taxes and spending may also be higher in places with relatively large poor or minority populations.

This model suggests that if larger communities are characterized by greater population heterogeneity, the political costs of raising taxes may be high if enough groups fear that too much of the additional spending will go to other groups. Political costs may also be high if officials in larger communities have greater uncertainty about voter preferences. Given risk aversion, they will then be less likely to propose tax and spending increases.

One possible consequence of falling property values may be to increase the political cost of raising taxes. I hypothesize that political costs will rise if falling property values are associated with shifts in the share of taxes paid by various groups of city residents. Any shifting of taxes among taxpayers implies that there are winners and losers. The losers pay higher taxes but receive no extra benefits, while the winners get a windfall. If the losers are more numerous or more politically powerful than the winners, the result of a shift in the tax base is likely to be heightened opposition to increased spending. In a number of cities the value of commercial property fell much more than the value of residential property, implying a shift in taxes from businesses to residents. There has also been a tendency in some cities for high-valued houses to decline at a much greater rate than low-valued houses. As a result of this pattern, property tax liabilities are shifted from business and high-income families to homeowners of relatively modestly valued houses, a group that in many cities is quite politically active.

Let me provide examples from three cities where declining property values appear to be associated with a shift in the share of property tax liabilities being levied on low- and moderate-income homeowners.

- In Boston, commercial property, primarily downtown office buildings, and high-value houses and condominiums fell in value much more than low-value residential property. While many commercial and high-value residential properties lost about a quarter of their value, low-value houses lost very little value.
- Using data on repeat sales in Los Angeles, Karl Case and Robert Shiller have calculated that in 1991 residential values for the one-third of houses with the highest prices dropped by 11 percent, while the values of the cheapest one-third of houses declined by 1 percent.
- Between 1987 and 1991 the assessed value of single-family

houses in Dallas fell by 14 percent, while during the same period the assessed value of industrial property declined by 33 percent (State of Texas 1992).

Voter resistance to higher taxes may also be increasing for several reasons not directly related to falling property values. Budgetary pressure in a number of states has led state governments to cut the amount of fiscal assistance going to city governments. For example, in Boston, state general-purpose aid in FY 1992 is 22 percent below its FY 1989 level. Substantial cuts in state aid have also occurred in a number of other states, including New York, Ohio, Minnesota, Maryland, and Michigan. As a consequence of these aid cuts, local revenue must be used to replace state revenue. As a result, city residents see their taxes going up but do not benefit from any corresponding increase in public services.[9] Again, the link between taxes and service provision has been weakened.

During the past ten years cities have had to respond to a number of new problems, such as homelessness, the AIDs epidemic, and the spread of crack-cocaine. Although it is likely that the majority of city residents believe that government has a responsibility to respond to these problems, the fact remains that much of the cost of the response must be borne by city residents. Cities respond directly to problems by adding newly targeted services—for example, the construction of shelters for the homeless. However, the growth of these new problems also tends to increase the costs to city governments of providing core city services such as police and fire protection, sanitation, and public health. The consequence of the city spending money in response to these problems is that city residents see their taxes increasing at the same time that the quality of the core city services declines or, in the best case, remains unchanged. Again, added taxes are not associated with added public services.

A rational response to these higher costs of providing city services may be to demand fewer services. In a study of local governments in Massachusetts, using 1980 data, Bradbury et al. (1984) statistically identified a set of community characteristics that are beyond the control of local officials yet lead to higher spending. Among the "cost factors" they identified were the population density, the crime rate, and the fraction of housing units built before 1940. In a recent study, again using Massachusetts data, Reschovsky and Schwartz (1992a) found that when 1991 data were analyzed most of the cost factors identified in the Bradbury et al study were not statistically significant determinants of local government spending. One explanation of their inability to identify cost factors is that voters have responded to the higher costs of public services by opposing spending increases. If this is in fact the case, then high values of the cost factors will no longer be associated with higher levels of city government spending.

A further reason why resistance to higher property taxes may be increasing is that the cost of the property tax has risen for many homeowners as a direct result of the Tax Reform Act of 1986 (TRA). As the property tax is deductible, itemizers are able to reduce their total tax burden by an amount equal to their property tax liability times their federal marginal tax rate. TRA reduced marginal tax rates and, by increasing the standard deduction and limiting some deductible items, substantially reduced the number of itemizers. On the margin these provisions raised the tax price of an additional dollar of property taxes. Reschovsky and Chernick (1989) have estimated that as a result of TRA the demand for public services in central cities in New York State and Massachusetts declined by a small amount, probably no more than 1 percent.

The property tax creates a substantial burden on low-income residents. In a recent paper Chernick and Reschovsky (1990) calculated that in 1988 the average property tax burden (measured as taxes relative to income) for families below the poverty line was 7 percent in Massachusetts and 8.8 percent in New York. Families with incomes between 100 and 150 percent of the poverty line had burdens of 4.2 and 5.3 percent in the two states. (These calculations assume that landlords are able to shift 75 percent of the property tax to their tenants.) These are heavy burdens for people with extremely low incomes. It would not be surprising if many of the growing number of low-income residents of our large cities would thus be opposed to all tax increases, even if they know that they will suffer from public service cutbacks.

It is interesting to note that even though residential real estate values have fallen dramatically in a number of cities, the value of most homes is considerably higher in real terms than it was ten years ago. I would like to suggest that this gain in wealth has not resulted, as we might expect, in an increase in demand for public services by homeowners. In fact, I think the argument can be made that many homeowners completely capitalized their unrealized gain. In other words, they assumed that market values couldn't decline, and they adjusted their consumption stream to reflect their new level of wealth. Thus, when values declined, they tended to react with anger. They felt ''entitled'' to the high values and believed they had suffered a real loss when property values dropped. One outlet for their frustration and anger has been city government. Hence, for all the reasons outlined, I conclude that the prospects for increasing property tax rates are extremely small.

Cutting Spending

There are four major strategies that city governments could follow to reduce total spending:

(1) Cities could take steps to increase the efficiency or productivity of public good provision. In many cases substantial cost savings can be realized by instituting relatively simple changes in procedures. However, the ability of public officials to realize even modest increases in productivity is often stymied by civil service regulations or union work rules. A recent example illustrates both the promise of productivity increases and the difficulty in achieving them. In New York City, recent recycling efforts have substantially reduced the volume of ordinary trash that must be collected. As a consequence, on many routes sanita-

tion workers are finishing their routes several hours early. Under current union work rules, the Sanitation Department is unable to reassign workers who finish routes early to other tasks, or to lengthen established trash collection routes. Sanitation workers must be paid for a full day's work even though they finish their routes several hours early. Although this situation has received extensive press coverage, negotiations to change these work rules have so far proved unsuccessful.

(2) The wages and benefits of city employees could be either cut or frozen. As wages comprise the largest single component of city government expenditures, this strategy has the potential to reduce substantially city spending. A number of cities, including Houston and Boston, have recently resorted to wage freezes. Very little is known about the consequences of cutting wages for municipal employees. There are indications that at least in some cities, public employee compensation is substantially more generous than private sector compensation for comparable positions.[10] In cases in which a city government pays a compensation premium over competitive private sector wage levels, it is likely that wage freezes will not jeopardize a city's ability to attract high-quality workers. The question arises, however, of what happens if public sector wages fall below private sector wages for comparable jobs. We know very little about public sector labor markets. In particular, we need to answer the following questions:

• How hard will it be to find qualified public employees if wages fall below wage levels in equivalent private sector jobs?
• Will wage and benefit reductions reduce the morale of public employees so that productivity will fall?
• Will all the young and well-educated workers depart, leaving a less efficient workforce?

(3) Public spending can clearly be reduced by eliminating some public services. In some cities there are few services that could be cut without placing substantial hardships on certain residents. In other cities, selective service reductions could probably be accomplished without causing significant hardship. For exam-

ple, Milwaukee still has behind-the-house trash collection; although its elimination may be politically difficult, it would create few real hardships. City officials face difficult decisions. On the one hand, opposition to tax increases may leave them with few options other than cutting public services. On the other hand, service cuts can be self-defeating if: (a) they lead a substantial number of people (presumably with middle- and upper-class incomes) to leave the city, or (b) they lead people to develop the attitude, "As the government isn't doing anything for me, why should I support higher taxes?"

(4) A number of authors have recently argued that substantial public sector resources can be saved through *privatization* (Savas 1987, Donahue 1989).[11] City governments could, and perhaps should, get out of the business of providing goods and services that are essentially private in nature. I am skeptical, however, that the use of private firms to provide the core services, those characterized by substantial externalities, will both maintain broad access to the services and result in substantial cost saving. It is particularly unlikely that efforts at privatization will reduce costs if privatization merely replaces a single public sector supplier with a single private sector supplier. There is more promise of achieving cost reductions if a competitive situation, with multiple providers, can be set up within a city.

Although in most large cities there exist real possibilities for reducing costs, it is important to realize that a number of factors in the urban environment are likely to result in rising costs over the next few years. The following list is not meant to be comprehensive, but it includes a number of developments that will probably affect a large number of cities:

• A number of cities have large amounts of unfunded pension liabilities. An aging workforce in some cities means that over the next decade, as public employees retire in growing numbers, a growing fraction of current revenue will have to be allocated to pension payments. As an example of the magnitude of this problem, in Philadelphia 55 percent of all firefighters will reach retirement age within the next five years (City of Philadelphia 1992).

• The recent flooding of the Chicago Loop has only served to highlight the fact that a number of large cities, especially in the Northeast and Midwest, will have to invest substantial resources in repairing and modernizing their public infrastructure. Although deferred maintenance is a common way of dealing with short-run fiscal crises, eventually resources must be spent in order to maintain the viability of public facilities.

• A growing problem in a number of cities is the presence of toxic wastes on a large number of city-owned properties. For example, over the years the city of Milwaukee has acquired through tax foreclosures a number of properties that at some point housed dry cleaners. Unfortunately, many of those properties are badly contaminated with highly toxic dry-cleaning chemicals. The city is left with the responsibility for the cleanup and with little chance of financial reimbursement from the long-departed former owners.

• Despite the rhetoric to the contrary, over the past decade the federal government has passed legislation that will impose a number of costly mandates on city governments. In particular, legislation regulating air and water pollution and providing rights for disabled persons will place substantial liabilities on many city governments during the 1990s.

Increasing the Use of Nonproperty Taxes and User Fees

Aside from the political difficulties associated with raising taxes, the potential for increasing nonproperty taxes and user fees varies across cities. Cities such as Boston and Milwaukee get almost all their locally raised revenue from the property tax. They would benefit from expanded revenue options but are restricted from using alternative taxes by state law. On the other hand, the potential for revenue diversification is limited in San Francisco and New York because those two cities already levy a wide range of local taxes and hence have limited room for expansion to alternative tax instruments.

Conclusion

The fiscal prospects for most large American cities are not good. Although the recent declines in the market value of real estate in many of the nation's large cities will not by themselves lead to devastating fiscal crises, the long-run fiscal prospects are poor because the gap between the costs of providing an adequate level of public services and the revenue-raising capacity of cities is likely to increase over time. I believe that cities will find it increasingly harder to raise taxes from their citizens. Despite the recent attention paid to the plight of cities as a result of the Los Angeles riots, the prospects of a substantial infusion of new state or federal money into cities are small.

Although it is hard to be optimistic about the long-run fiscal health of big cities, let me conclude by mentioning a few factors that may provide cities with needed rays of hope. First, demographic changes may favor cities. In particular, the number of young workers will decline over the next decade. This will probably lead to labor shortages that will drive up wages in relatively low-skill jobs, providing a mechanism for city residents, especially those now on welfare, to get into the labor force and out of poverty. Second, the growing congestion in the suburbs and the lack of infrastructure to deal with it may allow cities, with their existing public transit networks and infrastructure (like sidewalks), to regain appeal for both individuals and businesses. Third, it is possible that the growing momentum toward restructuring the American health-care system will result in shifting the burden of paying for the health-care needs of the poor completely away from state and local governments to the federal government. Finally, although falling housing prices worsen the fiscal condition of cities in the short run, lower prices may serve to reinvigorate city economies in the long run if they attract a new generation of people into central cities.

Notes

1. While some people suffer from the decline in real estate values, others benefit. The combination of lower mortgage interest rates and lower prices is

enabling people to become homeowners who were previously excluded from the housing market.

2. The most recent data on the market value of real property in city governments come from the *1982 Census of Governments.* Collection of these data was discontinued in the 1987 census.

3. I should point out that market values are not declining everywhere. For the most part, property values rose slightly in the Midwest during the 1980s and have continued to rise during the early 1990s. One indication of the regional variation in real estate markets is provided by data from the American Housing Survey, which indicate that while median gross rents increased between 1985 and 1989 at an annual rate of 2.4 percent in the Northeast and 1.2 percent in the West, they decreased at an annual rate of 0.6 percent in the Midwest and 1.3 percent in the South (Apghar 1991).

4. A good example is Philadelphia, one of the few large eastern cities where property values have not fallen. I don't pretend to be an expert on that city, but I think it is clear that while Philadelphia has severe fiscal problems, there are other cities in worse fiscal health. Philadelphia's fiscal problems have a lot to do with a recent history of weak and fragmented political leadership and hostile relationships between the city and the state government.

5. For a full discussion of consequences of alternative state-aid cutback strategies, see Reschovsky and Schwartz (1992b).

6. According to data compiled by the District of Columbia Department of Finance and Revenue, the effective residential property tax rate in the largest city in about half the states, was lower in 1990 than it was in 1981 (Government of the District of Columbia 1991).

7. Another example of the difficulty of obtaining voter approval to raise property taxes comes from Ohio, where increases in public school budgets cannot be adopted without explicit voter approval in a referendum. In Cleveland, despite repeated efforts to increase school spending, a school budget referendum has not been approved since the mid-1980s.

8. Although a reasonable model of intrametropolitan locational choices suggests that mobility is sensitive to the relative fiscal condition of the city rather than to tax rates alone, the visibility of the tax rates may lead city officials to overemphasize their importance. For example, in Milwaukee under Mayor John Norquist the central focus of the city's fiscal policy has been to reduce the city's mill rate each year. It should also be noted that in some metropolitan areas market values have declined more in the suburbs than in the central city, placing pressure on suburban communities to raise their tax rates.

9. Alternatively, city governments may choose not to replace state assistance. In that case, property taxes remain unchanged, but service levels are cut.

10. For example, in Philadelphia a recent study by the city controller and the Pennsylvania Economy League found that clerks and typists working for the city earned a premium over private sector compensation levels of 50 to 70 percent, janitors and cleaners a premium of nearly 50 percent, and security guards a premium of almost 85 percent (City of Philadelphia 1992).

11. For a well-balanced treatment of the privatization issue, see Gormley (1991).

References

Apghar, William C., Jr. 1991. "Housing the Nation's Poor." Paper prepared for presentation at the La Follette Institute Housing Conference. Madison: La Follette Institute of Public Affairs.

Bradbury, Katharine L. 1991. "Can Local Governments Give Citizens What They Want? Referendum Outcomes in Massachusetts." *New England Economic Review,* Federal Reserve Bank of Boston, May/June.

Bradbury, Katharine L. et al. 1984. "State Aid to Offset Fiscal Disparities Across Communities." *National Tax Journal* 37:2 (June).

Case, Karl E. 1991. "The Real Estate Cycle and the Economy: Consequences of the Massachusetts Boom of 1984–87." *New England Economic Review,* Federal Reserve Bank of Boston, September/October.

Case, Karl E., and Shiller, Robert J. 1988. "The Behavior of Home Buyers in Boom and Post-Boom Markets." *New England Economic Review,* Federal Reserve Bank of Boston, November/December.

CB Commercial. 1991. "Office Vacancy Index of the United States, December 31, 1991." Los Angeles: CB Commercial Real Estate Group.

Chernick, Howard. 1990. "Distributional Constraints on State Decisions to Tax." Paper presented at the 1990 National Bureau of Economic Research Summer Institute on State and Local Finance, Cambridge, Massachusetts.

Chernick, Howard. 1992. "Real Property Taxation in New York City: The Need for Immediate Reform." A report prepared by the City Project, New York, February.

Chernick, Howard, and Reschovsky, Andrew. 1990. "The Taxation of the Poor." *Journal of Human Resources* 25: 712–35.

City of Boston. 1991. *Property Tax Facts and Figures; Fiscal Year 1992 Revaluation.* Boston: Assessing Department, fall.

City of New York. 1992. "Press Release on 1992 Assessments, January 15, 1992." New York: Finance Department.

City of Philadelphia. 1992. *Five-Year Financial Plan, Fiscal Year 1992–Fiscal Year 1996.* Philadelphia: Office of the Mayor.

City of San Francisco. 1991. *Comprehensive Annual Financial Report, Fiscal Year 1990–91.* San Francisco: Controllers' Office.

Donahue, John D. 1989. *The Privatizational Decision: Public Ends, Private Means.* New York: Basic Books.

Gold, Steven D. 1992. "State Policies Affecting Cities and Counties in 1991: Shift and Shaft Federalism?" *Public Budgeting & Finance* 12 (Spring): 23–46.

Gormley, William T., Jr., ed. 1991. *Privatization and Its Alternatives.* Madison: University of Wisconsin Press.

Government of the District of Columbia. 1991. *Tax Rates and Tax Burdens in the District of Columbia: A Nationwide Comparison.* Washington, D.C.: Department of Finance and Revenue.

Inman, Robert P. 1989. "The Local Decision to Tax: Evidence from Large U.S. Cities." *Regional Science and Urban Economics* 19 (August): 455–91.

Ladd, Helen F., and Yinger, John. 1989. *America's Ailing Cities: Fiscal Health and the Design of Urban Policy.* Baltimore: Johns Hopkins University Press.

Ladd, Helen F., and Yinger, John. 1991. *America's Ailing Cities: Fiscal Health and the Design of Urban Policy,* Updated Edition. Baltimore: Johns Hopkins University Press.

Luce, Thomas F., and Summers, Anita A. 1987. *Local Fiscal Issues in the Philadelphia Metropolitan Area.* Philadelphia: University of Pennsylvania Press.

Mankiw, N. Gregory, and Weil, David N. 1989. "The Baby Boom, the Baby Bust, and the Housing Market." *Regional Science and Urban Economics* 19: 235–58.

McGuire, Therese J. 1985. "Are Local Property Taxes Important in the Intrametropolitan Location Decisions of Firms? An Empirical Analysis of the Minneapolis–St. Paul Metropolitan Area." *Journal of Urban Economics* 18: 226–34.

New York State Financial Control Board. 1991. *Staff Report: New York City Financial Plan FY 1992–1995,* August.

Oldman, Oliver, and Aaron, Henry. 1965. "Assessment-Sales Ratios Under the Boston Property Tax." *National Tax Journal* 18: 36-49.

Reschovsky, Andrew. 1979. "Residential Choice and the Local Public Sector: An Alternative Test of the Tiebout Hypothesis," *Journal of Urban Economics* 6: 501–20.

Reschovsky, Andrew, and Chernick, Howard. 1989. "Federal Tax Reform and the Taxation of Urban Residents." *Public Finance Quarterly* 17: 123–57.

Reschovsky, Andrew, and Schwartz, Amy Ellen. 1992a. "Evaluating the Success of Need-Based Aid in the Presence of Property Tax Limitations." *Public Finance Quarterly* 20: 489–506.

Reschovsky, Andrew, and Schwartz, Amy Ellen. 1992b. "The Impacts of Grant-in-Aid Cutbacks on Fiscal Disparities among Recipient Governments." In *Public Finance with Several Levels of Government,* Proceedings of the 46th Congress of the International Institute of Public Finance, Brussels 1990, ed. Rémy Prud'homme. The Hague: Foundation Journal Public Finance.

Savas, E.S. 1987. *Privatization: The Key to Better Government.* Chatham, NJ: Chatham House.

State of Texas, Office of the Comptroller. 1992. "1991 Property Value Study." Austin: Property Tax Division, Comptroller of Public Accounts.

U.S. Bureau of the Census. 1991. *City Government Finance,* Series GF. Washington, D.C.: Government Printing Office.

Wasylenko, Michael J. 1980. "Evidence of Fiscal Differentials and Intrametropolitan Firm Relocation." *Land Economics* 56: 337–49.

6

What Are the Limits of Government? What Are Its Obligations?

WILLIAM K. TABB

Introduction

The subject of this chapter is as broad as it is important. My task is similar to that of presenting a lawyer's brief, one that makes the case for the cities and their need to finance the costs of preserving what remains of civility and solidarity in urban America. In my argument, I first clarify the shift in mainstream urbanist thinking and national policymaking from what I call redistributive liberalism to neo-conservative reprivatization. Second, I present, in some detail, the data—the trends regarding fiscal stress and the changing role of the federal government—and relate these trends to larger developments in the national and international economy. I then introduce what I consider to be the major departure of the present study.

Without a reversal of current trends, the nation as a whole will become poorer and less able to compete internationally. The competitiveness discourse and the understanding we have of the Japanese cultural economy and governance institutions have important implications for shaking up our tired liberal-conservative debate on the urban fiscal crisis and the proper function of government. The usual cost-benefit analyses show that few traditional programs are economically efficient; this narrow definition of efficiency is part of the problem.

In the 1970s the dominant urban policy shifted from a redistributive liberalism to a neo-conservative privatization. At the highest levels of policymaking, government ceased to be seen as the agency for addressing market failures and providing the public goods needed to promote the general welfare. Government surely by the early 1980s was seen as the problem. Acceptance of such changes at the level of ideology (a shift in the general understanding of the proper role of the state with regard to issues of economic efficiency and equity) reflected changes in the economic base of the society: slower growth, a more unequal income distribution, and perhaps above all the perception that we had lost our competitiveness and were in relative economic decline. Thus, to ask about the obligations of the state as we approach the twenty-first century requires us to cast a wide net. This is particularly important at a time when the nation seems to have lost much of its faith in the future—the optimism that has characterized our country over most of its history.

It is not a very controversial contention that the cul de sac of racial animosity, unmet social needs, taxpayer revolt, and efforts to promote a mean and lean economy while maintaining a kinder, gentler nation have produced tensions that can be expected to worsen unless some new policy departure is forthcoming. The causes run deep, not simply in the American psyche, but also to the material base of our economy's insertion into the new world order. While there are good reasons for the prevailing pessimism, it is not impossible to explain coherently how we got where we are or to talk sensibly of how we might move to a better situation. This will require a public philosophy that privileges developmentalist state activities, redefines economic presuppositions in a socially more cohesive manner, and establishes a social movement capable of turning its desires into effective activity.

Although the academic divisions between urban studies and macroeconomic analysis are necessary for in-depth investigation of narrowly defined problems, when it comes to the fate of our cities, they stand in the way of looking at the Big Picture. For this task, we must develop a single analytic framework that will allow us to think about how we might act not only locally, but at the national level as well, within a context of a positive globalism. The quality of life in our cities cannot be separated from the success of our national economy. The faults of our urban policies at this time are integrally linked to larger failures. The politics of the debate must be examined in terms of: (1) how the increasingly internationalized elites view their home country; (2) the manner in which working-class and middle-class voters, who have been buffeted by the dislocations and downward economic mobility of the last two decades, conceptualize what is possible and desirable; and (3) how traditional themes of inclusion and social justice are interpellated in an increasingly internationalized economy.

Agglomeration economies and the quality of urban life have systematically been relegated to the background by the global concerns mentioned above, and yet the city as a site of production and consumption plays a crucial role in the competitiveness of the American economy. Face-to-face contact and the synergies of proximity affect information generation and exchange, the response time, and the quality of decisions made, as well as the possibilities of much cultural production and economies of scale in consumption. Such intangibles are important and cannot be easily replicated in a decentralized form. Interaction, planned and serendipitous, and location amenities that exist in historic city centers are important national resources. The extent to which social disintegration, violence, and pervasive disharmony undermine public order, civility, and solidarity diminishes our cities, and our cities are central to our future as a nation.

The framework of rebuilding America, reclaiming our edge, our sense of national purpose and shared community is now being discussed with some urgency. Labels become obsolete rapidly in such a context. For example, industrial policy, currently not a very popular programmatic departure, has potential in my view to reverse present destructive trends. Linking the ideological discussions, the economic theorization, the public philosophy debates, and government policymaking is not a simple matter. The assertion here is that it is the interplay between global changes in the political economy, the inadequate ways America has understood competitive markets and the role of the state, that must be interrogated if we are to look forward to a happier form of policymaking at the macro level and in terms of urban interventions.

I believe that the 1980s discourse of free markets has misunderstood much that is essential in the determination of international competitiveness and the wealth of nations. Readjusting our conceptual framework leads to a revision of urban policy as well. Such a perspective is not to advocate a return to a liberal welfare-state orientation on demand-side grounds but rather to relate a progressive interventionist agenda to supply-side strategies.

Liberal Interventionism in Historical Perspective

American thinking concerning intergovernmental relations was shaped during the long period from the New Deal through the Great Society in which demand-side economics privileged spending and redistribution as the engine of development in a relatively closed national economy. The hegemonic political coalition of this half century was the liberal-labor alliance, which included local developers and corporate leaders in mass production industries for whom state spending was accepted as supportive of continued national economic expansion and their own narrower economic interests. Thus, even after public housing came to serve a predominantly inner-city black clientele, for example, the lobbying strength of the construction interests involved kept funds flowing, far longer than one might have expected given the strength of the social coalitions supporting such a program. The liberal corporate elites likewise continued to favor Keynesianism until the stagflation crisis of the 1970s indicated that the old formula was no longer working and profit rates would continue to decline unless there was some new departure. But while it lasted, liberal Keynesianism gave the economy quite a run. The alliance of self-interest and social vision in the first half of the postwar era formed a political basis for a growth economy.

The form such stimulation took, whether the federal highway program from the mid-1950s with its primary multiplier impacts in housing and consumer durables, or military expenditures, shaped national politics and regional development patterns. State spending, economic growth, and a commitment to social justice seemed to go together. The pattern of federal spending, job creation, and rising incomes, however, did not prevent what came to be known as the urban crisis, because it relied on the trickle-down understanding of the multiplier concept. Spending would beget spending, job creation would produce more jobs. Unfortunately, before full employment was reached, worrisome inflation occurred. In the increased internationally competitive climate of the 1970s, fiscal stimulus was also likely to "leak" abroad, creating balance-of-payment problems. And with the global marketplace beckoning, U.S.-based multinational corporations increasingly invested abroad rather than at home.

Domestic political problems arose as well. For example, while the 1960s War on Poverty and Great Society programs were originally conceived in terms of job creation, they also sought to build community coherence in inner-city areas and to involve residents to the maximum feasible extent. This laudable democratic impulse of inclusion was always contested by more conservative forces on ideological and political grounds and by many mayors and governors for the pragmatic reason that such an approach bypassed their authority. In addition, such programs could not be funded without increasing taxes, and with an unpopular war in Vietnam moving into overdrive, the Johnson administration promised more than it could deliver. Thus, the 1960s ushered in an era of stagflation. In a period of slow growth, economic uncertainty, and taxpayer rebellion, redistributive liberalism was ready to be replaced by a neo-conservative privatization.

The connection between jobs and adequate income and a better quality of urban life seemed clear for much of our history. In the New Deal and Great Society eras, this awareness was met with programmatic responses. In 1937 the Roosevelt administration's National Resources Committee expressed this relation, declaring that:

> Because many of the most acute and persistent problems of the city cannot be solved until the fundamental issue of adequate and secure income is met, the Committee urges that efforts already made by Government, industry, and labor toward raising the level of family income and increasing economic security be continued and intensified.

In the New Deal era, the need to act was obvious. The support of interventionist policies increased as it was understood that only the federal government could address these problems successfully. Today, as the nation once again faces a deep crisis, there is an unwillingness to act forcefully to address economic and social problems. This represents a relatively new departure. From the 1930s to the 1970s, activist government had meant Keynesian-state spending policies with a redistributional caste. But in the post-1970s, job creation was to be sought by unleashing the power of free markets to stimulate employment and raise income. This reversed a trend that had until then seemed integral to modern capitalism. Tax cuts and government spending, of course, continued, but the tax reductions went to upper-income Americans, the spending increases went to a military buildup, and, since the federal budget was stressed, social spending was dramatically cut. Government was no longer the solution to social problems. It was to get out of the way of the private market. In brief, the rising federal deficit caused by these policies was given as the reason nothing could be done for middle-class citizens or the poor. We could no longer afford such government generosity in times of budget deficits.

Before the 1980s, increases in total government spending and even larger increases by state and local jurisdictions, thanks to federal assistance, seemed a natural evolution as the nation grew richer. It was understood that fiscal stimulus promoted economic well-being and economic growth. Government spending's share could be expected to increase, and so it did. Total federal spending as a percentage of GNP more than doubled between the 1920s and the 1960s. Between 1960 and 1980 federal spending (excluding defense, interest payments, and grants to states and localities) almost doubled again.

Through this period the case was made, and was widely accepted, that there was not only no conflict between economic growth and progressive social policy, but that growth through equity was also economically efficient. After the Vietnam War, policymakers began to see a "great trade-off" (Okun 1975) between equity and efficiency. By the late 1970s, the view that there was a conflict between efficiency and equity increasingly gained currency. The orthodoxy of the 1980s was that growth must precede equity. The impact of this change on urban policy was profound. Cities were expected to be entrepreneurs, offering incentives to attract businesses to locate and to remain within their jurisdictions. Local spending was constrained by the local tax base to an even greater extent than in the past when revenue sharing had been significant. Localities were required to promote capital accumulation through greater reliance on the market. Deregulation and privatization, contracting out, cutting social spending, and limiting wages and benefits of government workers became standard operating procedure for national, state, and local governments.

Yet the impact of these changes suggests that fend-for-yourself federalism and extension of enterprise culture to the local state needs to be examined in social efficiency terms.[1] This involves an exploration of the varied meanings of other key terms: flexibility, competition, and profit. This conceptual rethinking of the dominant economic assumptions of the 1980s is integral to the task of addressing our urban fiscal crisis. Because the problems of cities are derived from larger socioeconomic structural relationships, they must be considered in a context that is large enough to encompass their ultimate and not simply their proximate causes.

In an era of intensified international competition and slower global growth, efficiency and productivity have replaced social justice and equity. To put matters crudely, globally oriented elites, most especially in the United States but to varying degrees elsewhere as well, have weaker ties to the masses in their own countries. As their networks and communities have become global, they have seceded. In an era of "laissez faire cosmopolitanism," to use Robert Reich's (1992, chapter 5) phrase, cutting back the public sector and supply-side incentives defines national priorities and constrains urban policy of the more traditional sort.

Conservative Politics

In the 1980s, conservative politicians made three important discoveries. The first was that while Americans overwhelmingly continued to support the specific programs that constituted the welfare state, they also felt they were not getting their money's worth from government and favored lowered taxes and less overall government spending. At the national level the Reagan-Bush administration moved decisively to cut taxes (as it turned out, in ways that only brought lower taxes to the upper 20 percent and especially to the richest 1 percent), forcing cuts in social programs, overwhelmingly those that benefitted the poorest Americans. Their second discovery was the domestic political implications of internationalization. Corporate elites who had accepted Keynesianism, trade unionism, and the welfare state increasingly held a global perspective in which lower taxes, lower state spending, and lower wages were seen as the means to create profits in the global economy. Faced with intensified international competition and seeking export markets, they relied less on cooperative unions at home and more on soaring production abroad. In search of world markets, rather than stimulating domestic ones, they changed their basic orientation to one that challenged the role of the state in the economy. Third, conservative politicians discovered that the Southern Strategy expounded most prominently by Kevin Phillips in the Nixon years, had blossomed into a Sunbelt-Suburban Coalition that was in direct opposition to big cities and their darker-skinned, Democratic-voting, New Deal–oriented citizens. This new coalition made it possible to win elections by being anti-urban, anti-union and anti-black. The special interests, a term that had not long before meant the corporate rich came instead to mean progressive social change organizations from the ACLU "criminals' lobby" to labor unions and the women's movement.

The conservative ascendancy at the national level was made possible by voter perceptions that War on Poverty–type programs were not achieving their goals; worse still, a growing number of voters associated those programs with increasing crime rates, welfare dependency, the erosion of the family, and babies born out of wedlock. There was an ever more apparent public resentment toward special privileges to "them" that were paid for out of "our" tax dollars. For many, these tax/transfers were essentially going to people whose behavior was more and more troubling. The cause-and-effect relation promised by the liberals, that investment in the poor would pay dividends for America, did not materialize. In a time of stagnant or declining real income, plant closings, and layoffs, of just getting by and of not really making it, the tax revolt and the anger that fueled the Reagan and Bush campaigns and, more recently, the David Duke and Patrick Buchanan campaigns, moved American politics to the right and kept it there.

We cannot brush aside this systemic change by simply saying that Mr. Bush's handlers used "quotas" as effectively as Ronald Reagan used "welfare queens," and that we are now reaping the results of this maelstrom. There was more than an appeal to a not-so-covert racism at work there. As Thomas Bryne Edsall (1992, 7) has written:

> Willie Horton, busing, and quotas draw on latent and overt racism;

> but they also address such central and legitimate concerns as neighborhood security, fairness in the workplace, and what many see as the struggle to maintain the values of hard work, personal responsibility and initiative, and perseverance.

This period of stagnation, cutbacks and givebacks, and a negative sum game that most in society had to play brought out the underside of politics. The rich may be getting richer, but it is the unruly urban underclass who are perceived as the immediate threatening problem. The liberals, on the other hand, appear to coddle criminals and call the white majority racist. Neither position endeared liberals to the voters and indeed appeared to make things worse for America. On a broader plane, the Bush campaign in 1988 was designed to show that the momentum of such programs was "endangering the safety and the stability of the larger community. Bush made much of the possible social and financial consequences of the movements on behalf of the rights of previously marginalized groups . . . " (Edsall 1992, 10). Many scared Americans resonated to such a critique.

From a left perspective, such increased costs represented partial compensation for historical wrongs to these groups and an inadequate effort to redress policies to more closely approximate just relations. The chant popular among some militants, "No justice, no peace," represented a stark formulation of such a position. It was a response to the contention that if they were to behave and stop complaining, everything would be better.

Unfortunately, the 1980s prosperity did not improve conditions in the inner cities. From a social systems perspective, it would be difficult to take issue with Anthony Downs's (1985, 289) judgment that "the white dominated U.S. society has clearly chosen to create and maintain two racially separate and unequal societies, as the Kerner Commission feared it might." From the viewpoint of many, possibly most, America's minorities had been given an equal chance, but they were not taking it. They didn't want to do the hard work of making their own way. They had serious attitude problems. They thought of themselves as victims and wanted society to give them preferential treatment, while the white majority had to work for what it received.

From Urban Crisis to Fiscal Strain

Urbanists have responded to these developments by first facing the economic and political inadequacies of 1960s-type urban revitalization strategies. Some have made a transition in their thinking from viewing the urban fiscal crisis as an inability to meet local needs to viewing it as an inability to balance the budget. Those who have taken the latter position see the problem as one of political will by local officials to make the necessary programmatic adjustments.[2] Those who continue to speak out for revenue sharing and social programs to help those most in need also focus on political will, but for them it is the failure at the federal level to address social suffering and urban decay that is still the pivotal issue. Accepting cutbacks is to accept defeat in a society in which the resources to address these problems continue to exist even if such reallocation appears not to be feasible under present arrangements.

The problem with the view that "policies must adapt to this new urban reality" is the clearly unacceptable nature of that reality. As my colleague Harry Levine (1991, 13) has lamented: "The United States needs a Marshall Plan for the cities. Instead, for the last ten years we've had what might appropriately be termed a Dresden Plan." If Levine's lament is to be heeded, the nature of such a Marshall Plan must be carefully considered. Simulation models of anti-decline interventionist programs show that they are not cost effective. The Bradbury, Downs, and Small (1981) modeling of the Cleveland Standard Metropolitan Statistical Area, which includes creating jobs, expanding federal welfare payments, rehabilitating housing, improving transportation, even merging city and county governments fiscally and purposefully restraining suburban growth, shows such steps slow but do not halt the loss of jobs and the movement of people out of the city.

In any case, spending money to revitalize cities, as in Model Cities and other anti-decline programs, in the current climate is not politically possible. Indeed, although they have probably not studied the results of Jay Forrester's *Urban Dynamics* (1969) model, many mayors know that tearing down housing in which the poor live is the best way to raise per capita income in their cities (it drives the poor out of their jurisdictions).[3]

By the mid-1980s, a new urban "realism" declared that saving the industrial city and transforming poverty-stricken neighborhoods was not only impossible, it was also undesirable. Paul E. Peterson (1985), the principal advocate of this new orthodoxy, declares: "Quite apart from political changes that have occurred in Washington, economic and social changes have moved so far that reversing their direction no longer seems feasible or even desirable." It is not possible, in this view, to make the case for greater spending to rebuild our cities on economic grounds as we traditionally understand such calculations. Within the usual efficiency framework, attempting to recreate what had been and no longer is would be wasteful and impossible to achieve with even the most generous allocation of funding that the most enthusiastically pro–older cities regime could muster. It is just not realistic to think in terms of physical rebuilding, because we live in a market economy, and these areas will remain unable to sustain competitive development. The social fabric and human capital resources to support such investment are not there. Constructively addressing the fate of our cities will require a new way of thinking.

Thus, there has been a marked shift from an urban fiscal paradigm focused on the problems of urban decline and especially urban poverty (which presumed an important federal role) to a focus on urban fiscal strain, which proposes that local governments must adapt to their environment by reducing expenditures and living within market-imposed restraints like any other business. In this shift there has been little disagreement about the facts. In the second half of the 1980s, a period of record economic expansion for the U.S. economy, states and localities suffered a dramatic loss of capacity to meet their fiscal obligations. In 1986 states and localities ran a $5.6 billion surplus. By 1990 they had a $33.2 billion deficit, which continued to increase in the early 1990s, as well over half of all states found themselves running deficits (Sullivan 1991, Rubin 1990).[4] In the liberal urban literature, such developments would have signaled the need for more federal assistance (Ladd 1990). In the public choice orthodoxy of the 1980s, neo-liberal and neo conservative urbanists "discourage the federal government from attempting to give aid to cities for programs they can best do themselves" (Peterson 1985, 25).

Federal decentralization has meant increased burdens on levels of government least able to bear them, an intensification of the differences in the quality of life of those who live in cities, and greater suffering at the lower end of the income scale as the rich further remove themselves from the life space of the rest of the nation. The vicious cycle imposed by fend-for-yourself federalism is clear enough. It is akin to the policies advocated by the International Monetary Fund to third world debtors: No pain, no gain. Austerity is the unavoidable consequence of economic stability.

Faced with rising expenditure needs brought on by slow economic growth and a secular increase in costs associated with intense social problems, cities must raise taxes; unfortunately, this causes more affluent taxpayers to move and further diminishes the tax base. Help from the federal level is not forthcoming because of the popular understanding of self-interest and the political arithmetic a suburban majority imposes.

The most influential urbanist literature has followed the election results to a remarkable degree. While urbanists need to think about how the center of gravity of the professional literature changed over the 1980s and evaluate the extent to which the new emphases are justified, this rethinking does not take place in the ivory tower. Real world forces intrude and influence intellectual production. In 1992, the nation experienced one of the more dismal episodes of its quadrennial pastime of selecting a president.

The Republicans ignored urban issues almost totally except to blame liberal cities like New York for creating their own problems (leading the *New York Times* to accuse the Grand Old Party of attempting to make New York City "the Willie Horton of the 1992 campaign"). National Democratic Party politics did not attack cities but instead focused on middle-class relief. During the primaries, the major contenders for the Democratic presidential nomination abandoned attempts to address problems of poverty and the declining quality of life in the nation's inner cities. "The candidates seem almost oblivious to the crisis conditions—in education, housing, health care, crime, AIDs, drug abuse—afflicting African-American communities across the country" (Muwakkil 1992, 2). The trendy label "compassion fatigue" (many voters are reported "tired" of poor people) is I think misleading. Surveys show overwhelmingly that Americans are troubled by homelessness and other economic and social ills. They are pessimistic, however, that anyone knows how to realistically address those ills. No longer do we have a general consensus to seek solutions to particular problems; now the consensus is that we simply cannot afford to address these problems. While some observers see an evolutionary (or devolutionary) trend in our inner cities, which are reverting to jungles, it is possible to suggest that the material base of the worsening economic environment is far stronger than the "hypersexuality" of "hyperaggressive," violence-prone monkeys, as a Bush administration official once suggested.[5]

The Federal Role

Federal grants comprised 27 percent of state and local spending in 1978 and 17 percent in 1988 (Gold 1990). Considering cities alone, between 1977 and 1990 federal aid was reduced by 64 percent. Between 1980 and 1990 non–Social Security domestic programs and services as a share of GDP were cut by 25 percent. Over the decade, federal spending on education and training dropped by 40 percent as a share of GDP. The basic cash assistance program for the poor, AFDC (Aid to Families with Dependent Children), fell 42 percent in purchasing power between 1970 and 1991 and then continued to fall further in 80 percent of the states in fiscal 1992. States also cut medical assistance and housing programs for the poor. In 1989, after an economic expansion that lasted six years, a record peacetime growth experience, more people were poor than in 1979. Comparing 1992 to 1977, the richest 1 percent of taxpayers contributed 30 percent less of their income in taxes at the federal level. At the state level also, when taxes were introduced, they were more regressive than the tax system they replaced. Spending priorities also shifted. One of the most dramatic and telling is the shift from schools to prisons. Nationally, state and local spending on prisons and corrections rose by 78 percent between 1977 and 1989 as a share of GDP, while state and local spending on schools fell by 5.3 percent. We suffer from an urban pessimism. The data is well rehearsed, and there is little doubt as to the trends.[6]

The repeated assertions that giving more responsibility (without giving increased resources) to state and local governments leads to greater democracy and responsiveness to citizen participation wear thin. The constraints under which such "people's power" is exercised force a Hobson's Choice of negative sum solutions. The notion that a smaller, less interventionist government sector encourages private enterprise and thus superior economic performance fails the reality test, since the hallmark of national political discourse over the last decade or more demonstrates that the states where economic performance is strong are the very states that have employed an active public sector. While the American trend has been to redistribute income upward as an economic incentive, the developmentalist states have used governance powers to encourage economic growth more directly and in boldly industrial policy ways. Education and training, infrastructure, and targeted research and development have been seen as important tools in an economic strategy; they have not been viewed as wasted expenditures by a bloated state. We will return to the significance of this contrast in approach.

The burden of added responsibility shifted from the federal to the subnational level, and the share of resources that was raised by these jurisdictions increased. State and local governments' share of resources rose from 43 percent in 1980 to 48 percent in 1989. Reliance of state and local governments on federal grants fell from 21.6 percent to 16.2 percent of their total revenues between 1977 and 1986 (Bahl and Sjoquist 1990, 325; Mullen 1990). The programs most severely affected were ones most important to the nation's future well-being, especially those that affected the young.

For the nation as a whole, public funding to train and retrain workers fell by more than 50 percent in the 1980s, from $13.2 billion to $5.6 billion, according to the Center on Budget Priorities (Reich 1992, 258). While there is increased recognition that public spending can be directly and especially indirectly productive (Aschauer 1989, Munnell 1990), the entire framework of conventional economic and political thinking in contemporary America leads corporations increasingly to make conflicting and harsh demands on governments at all levels. Politically they call for increased public investment in the name of competitiveness. Privately they demand tax concessions. In both cases they threaten relocation and job loss to the jurisdiction. As a result, the corporate share of local property tax revenues declined from 45 percent in 1957 to 16 percent thirty years later, according to the Advisory Commission on Intergovernmental Relations. Yet, in spite of this, an increasing number of U.S. corporations have moved their operations.

Since 1977 no state has increased spending on education as a share of its total expenditures; that is, average spending on education has declined as a proportion of total expenditures. It is true that declining enrollments may be a factor here, but in an era in which U.S. children's test scores are an issue in the competitiveness discussion, the trend seems ominous. Even more frustrating is that the areas of increased expenditures, such as criminal justice and health care, do not reflect a higher quality of life.

This is further complicated by the increasingly regressive

overall tax system and the abrogation of former federal service provision accommodations, which exacerbate interjurisdictional competition, reduce tax capacity, and impose harsh choices on state and local governments. State legislatures that are controlled by a coalition of suburban and rural interests in a time of economic stagnation have little ready cash for or interest in central cities. Looking at these trends, it is difficult to disagree with Bahl and Sjoquist's (1990, 338) conclusion that "expenditure reduction and heightened city-suburban competition for a smaller pool of state aid is almost certain to result."

Declining federal, state, and local spending to help address and reverse inequality in America coincides with two related patterns: the decline in real income for most working Americans, and the loss of U.S. competitiveness in global markets. The interrelationship of these three trends will be demonstrated in the remainder of this essay.

The Eclipse of the American Dream

Average real wages in the United States peaked in 1973, fell, briefly regained 1973 levels in 1979, and fell again. Consequently, on the *average*, we have been treading water for two decades; some of us are drowning, however, while a few boats are sailing high on the waves. For most of us, housing costs, medical expenses, and college tuition have increased sufficiently compared to our income to put the basics of middle-class life beyond our means. The 1990s have begun with a different kind of recession. It is more widespread than the sectorally and regionally concentrated downturns of the postwar era. When General Motors announces it will have to let go half of its 1985 workforce by 1995 and IBM announces serious cutbacks, few people feel their own jobs are safe. Cutbacks are not simply in blue-collar jobs but in management and professional categories as well.

In 1990 and 1991, the number of very poor families on welfare increased more than it did in the previous sixteen years. In 1992, the presidential candidates campaigned in New Hampshire in the nation's first primary of the election year, they faced unusually hostile voters. Welfare cases in that predominantly conservative Republican, white working-class state had risen by over 75 percent in 1990 and 1991. People who only a short time earlier had blamed the victims for their poverty and assured the poor that all they needed to do was to "work" their way out of poverty and become self-sufficient now demanded federal action for themselves. As the cuts in welfare state spending proceeded, pain was becoming more widespread in America. Nationally, the benefits paid to AFDC recipients had fallen to half their mid-1970s levels in real terms. States from New Jersey to California essentially punished single mothers and newborn illegitimate children. Some states went so far as to punish parents if their kids did not attend school. Taxpayers were desperate. Their own incomes were falling, and in their anger and desperation they struck out at those less fortunate.

Congressional Budget Office data show that from 1977 through 1991 only the top 20 percent of households enjoyed real income gains. For the top 1 percent, real income more than doubled. At the same time, the top 1 percent paid 30 percent less in taxes in 1992 than in 1977. The irony is that if the wealthy had not enjoyed these tax cuts and if taxes had been what they were prior to the Reagan-Bush years, domestic expenditure cutbacks would not have been necessary. The argument that the rich would invest and create jobs for the rest of us and that benefits would trickle down has not proved true. The stagnant economy and the loss of competitiveness created conditions quite different from the "utopian" world promised under supply-side economics. Workers' wages increased from an average of $136 a week for nonsupervisory production workers in 1972 to $359 a week in 1991. These workers were not, however, better off. After it is adjusted for inflation, their average income had fallen 9 percent. Between 1980 and 1990, 80 percent of American families lost ground. As Kevin Phillips (1991, 10) rather dramatically, but accurately, has written: "No parallel upsurge of riches has been seen since the late nineteenth century, the era of the Vanderbilts, Morgans and Rockefellers."

The United States is not the only nation in the world to experience falling or stagnant real income. Gross National Product per capita in the industrialized nations has slowed dramatically from the up phase of the postwar long-wave cycle (from 1950 to 1973), when the annual change was 3.6 percent, to the 1973–89 period, when it was only 2 percent. This represents a drop of 45 percent. This overall slowdown was sharp and universal (Magdoff 1992, 7, Table 1). Over the past decade, the United States, however, has set several dubious records. We now have the fastest-growing rate of income inequality in our history, and this poor performance ranks us at the bottom of the advanced nations of the world.

The Negative Sum Debate

While the need for "liberal" programs is evident, Thomas Bryne Edsall and Mary D. Edsall (1991, 287–88) have argued that liberals have been successfully portrayed as out of step with the majority concerns of today's electorate. In a period of conservative ascendancy, it is said that liberals—with a capital L—lack the tools or the will to confront the weakness of their own analysis and world view. It is useful to quote the Edsalls at some length, because they set out this perspective well:

> This debate is likely to become harsher as global competition intensifies—competition providing little or no room for traditional Democratic policies sheltering the disadvantaged. Intensified international competition will exert increasingly brutal pressure on America's economic and political systems, and on policies offering special protection, preferences or subsidies to groups within the population—whether they be ethnic or racial minorities, unskilled workers, prisoners, elected officials, the elderly, the disabled, AIDs victims, or single mothers.
>
> At stake in all of this is something far more important than partisan victory. First, stagnation at the bottom half of the income distri-

bution, together with the poverty, disappointment, and rage of America's disadvantaged minority population, threatens our social order. Secondly, at stake is our sense of ourselves as inhabiting an intelligible moral universe, committed to a form of social and economic organization that offers at least rough justice to its citizens in exchange for their participation. And thirdly, at stake is the American experiment itself, endangered by a rising tide of political cynicism and alienation, and by basic uncertainties as to whether or not we are capable of transmitting a sense of inclusion and shared citizenship across an immense and diverse population.

The problem from a macroeconomic perspective is that in order to attract footloose capital from other jurisdictions, each country has to reduce its wages and public services, increase its incentives and subsidies, and see living standards of its working people erode. At the end of the twentieth century, the competitiveness system is between governments and among workers. It boils down to a negative sum game of slow growth and contraction. The underconsumptionist undertow cannot be addressed by cities that must act as entrepreneurs competing among themselves.

The big gains in value added come from knowledge-intensive innovation, which reconceptualizes and restructures production processes and outputs. Much of both the blue-collar and the white-collar staffs of American corporations do work that can be, and is being, designed out. Layoffs at our largest corporations not only have a great deal to do with slower global growth and attempts to increase competitiveness, but they are also attributable to the rise of flexible production. The productivity of many employees in Fordist organizations is growing more slowly than the wages the workers receive. The standardized tasks that remain can be shipped abroad to lower-wage areas (Drucker 1991). Increasingly Americans have three choices: work smarter, work at worse paying jobs, or not work at all. Is there a way to gain these increases in productivity while minimizing the social dislocations they cause? Yes, there is.

Under such conditions global Keynesianism should have wide

appeal. Increasing wages and public sector spending would be possible if it were coordinated on an international basis. If it were not, any nation that pursues such a policy would quickly find itself with balance-of-payment problems. There is also a need for internationally binding arrangements that lead to a leveling up instead of a leveling down of living standards. Policies that increase investment in human resources and in infrastructure are necessary to provide guidance and rules for corporate behavior to stimulate both growth and productivity. A new international regime that puts social justice high on the agenda would allow for more balanced economic growth. It could also diminish counterproductive interjurisdictional negative sum competition.

The Urban Crisis As a Competitiveness Issue

When we look at competitiveness problems, the key concerns are usually listed as raising savings rates, increasing R&D, and reforms to discourage short-term profitability from dominating corporate decision making. These are not easy concerns to address. There are other issues, those of crime, poverty, and education, that are also competitiveness issues. The latter set of problems in fact may be more important. If this second set of concerns is faced squarely and dealt with, the social cohesion necessary for a successful national industrial policy would be achieved. If our national governance structures and policies are unable to develop effective responses to these social problems, the United States as an economic entity faces stagnation and the prospects of massive capital flight.

It is possible, of course, that if the nation does not address these issues effectively, a smaller enclave economy within the territory of the United States will prosper as a globally important island in a sea of decline. It will exist behind moats keeping the majority of our own citizens out, excluding them from the good life, which will be reserved for the elite and those working for the privileged strata. Signs of this trajectory are evident. The continuation of this scenario dooms the United States as we have known it. The United States will be diminished, because, as Hisashi Owada, Japan's vice minister for foreign affairs, has said, "The power to control social cohesion in domestic society is becoming even more important than physical power" (Getler 1991, 22).

The first point in the rethinking required in urban policy is to recast the discussion in just this way. It is not only a matter of elemental justice to meet the needs of the hungry, to house the homeless, and so on, although a country that does not understand this is in danger of losing its soul,[7] but it is a matter of the nation's economic future as well.

American views of market efficiency are static. The allocation of existing resources is central to our neo-classical tradition in economics. In contrast, the Japanese view of markets as a source of growth calls attention to the role of government in economic affairs, which is quite different. It is not about regulating to en- sure efficient allocation of existing resources and staying out of the way of market forces, but of supplying incentives and struc- turing markets to maximize growth. The Japanese have a more sophisticated, modern reading of Adam Smith's "functions of government." They see providing education and infrastructure as the highest priorities. Their inclusive, group-oriented society in- corporates citizens, using their talents in a collective effort to build the nation. The Japanese are not without their faults, to be sure, and their understanding of social efficiency, while in ad- vance of our own, is still insufficient; but they are not tyrannized by the short-run bottom line, and they have over a very long period put the nation ahead of individual profiteering. As Chal- mers Johnson (1987, 422) has written, "For the Japanese, the concept of 'market' refers primarily to the most effective form of social organization for eliciting entrepreneurship from the pub- lic." We might add that their conception of entrepreneurship is also far broader than ours. It includes the institutionalization of continuous change within structures, which are organized to ac- commodate rapid diffusion of new ideas and better practices.

Development theorists have long understood that the fundamental problem of development is not so much a matter of addressing the relation between known costs and known benefits but in generating and energizing human action. Decades ago, development theorists could look at the poorer nations and say whether development would take place or not hinged on whether a nation had a "building mentality" or a "milking mentality." Looking at the United States in the same light, this distinction is central. To what extent is new value created through investment, as economists define that term (the creation of physical and human capital that will increase our ability to produce output in the future)? To what extent is money made by rearranging assets so as to deploy them to achieve a short-term gain at the expense of the long run? Are we generating and energizing constructive human activities on the part of our citizens? Is social knowledge being applied to planning our future in a constructive fashion?

The Idealized Japanese Model As Counterpoint

From a Japanese perspective, industrial policy is an elastic concept. As Hiroya Ueno (1983, 34) writes:

> Unlike traditional fiscal and monetary policies, industrial policy demonstrates no clear relationship between its objectives and the means of attaining them. Its conception, content, and forms differ, reflecting the stage of development of an economy, its natural and historical circumstances, international conditions, and its political and economic situation, resulting in considerable differences from nation to nation and from era to era.[8]

In a Japan ruled by a cohesive capitalist leadership, the Liberal Democratic Party, working closely with the developmentalist state planners, such industrial planning can be a flexible tool. Tactics may differ over time and among situations. They may be influenced by shifts in ideological currents, some of which blow in from the West; but the goal of industrial policy remains as constant as the goals of monetary and fiscal policy. The tools and the concepts are contingent. Japan's effort to seek a place in the sun is blatantly protectionist. The Japan that has reached parity with the West can be more favorable to free trade. A Japan that seeks to build productive capacity in its major markets around the world can be more catholic than the pope, advocating free trade and even practicing it far more rigorously than the United States itself. Industrial policy is about increasing international competitiveness. International competitiveness, as students of Japanese industrial policy have shown, is about organizational inventiveness. Industrial policy properly conceived is about developing new and better forms of organization. To say that industrial policy is about distorting markets, creating disincentives, and disallowing market outcomes is, of course, as true as saying the reverse. Creating desirable incentives within which individual choices are made in the general interest is what good industrial policy is about.

For our purposes it is not necessary to recount how Japan has protected its domestic markets, allowed cooperation and encouraged competition among its firms, provided low-cost financing and export subsidies, underwritten the costs of research and development, and offered other forms of assistance.[9] The particular forms of proactive developmentalist policies are not integral to a definition of industrial policy.

It is difficult to exaggerate the depth of the changes that would be required for the United States to develop a successful set of policies that would allow us to approximate, in our own cultural economy, measures that would be as effective for us as Japan's developmentalist state has been for that nation. We would have to induce changes in our social consciousness, politics, and sense of national purpose; redouble our efforts at worker training and formal education; and develop an inclusive and cooperative stance toward community. To be successful, all of these elements must be involved. Most experts are skeptical. They believe we could never do it. But there are severe consequences of trying to muddle through without an industrial policy that seeks to rebuild America as a society and as an economic entity.

The United States has been described by Michael Porter, the Harvard Business School's leading light on the competitiveness issue, as having been "drifting for at least a decade."[10] There is no indication, one might add, that the nineties will be any better. Indeed, there are reasons to think they will be a lot worse. The United States badly needs to think strategically. Unfortunately, economists here will, by and large, like their English counterparts in the analogous situation a century ago, maintain allegiance to the virtues of the unfettered market. If the free market theorists win the debate, there is no reason to think that the growth gap between the United States and Japan will narrow except perhaps by Japanese ownership claims on America continuing to grow to the point that they bring us kicking and screaming into modernity in a manner we may find painful to our pride and limiting to our autonomy.

The decay of the American social fabric has come about in large measure because of the loss of national coherence under the force of internationalizing economic pressures. The demise of family and community bemoaned by social conservatives and others is in large measure the result of successful privatization of the accumulation process in the context of a more open world economy. The uneven development that results from sudden shifts in where and how production takes places leaves whole regions devastated, large numbers of people unprepared for the needs of new job market conditions, and local governments unable to make up deficits caused by privatization. This has been exacerbated by reduced revenue sharing from the central government, which is set on making markets more flexible and capital more mobile. Economic management under such conditions has become less, not more, effective. The failure of mainstream macroeconomics, in both its Keynesian and its monetarist versions, has created such a vacuum that theorists have returned to the premise that macroeconomics must be built on micro foundations. In the United States this has meant freer markets and less state intervention.

In the Japanese system, bureaucratic guidance, while it has

been insufficiently mindful of many aspects of social need and rightly criticized for its single-minded pursuit of growth, has been effective in structuring incentives for major actors. The burden of the present essay has been to suggest the superiority of this aspect of the Japanese solution. It takes for granted the constraining force of the globalization process but accommodates to it through activist policies. In the United States, macro policies first ignored the global constraints and then capitulated totally to what was seen as the free market–free trade imperative. Indeed, this was the downfall of Keynesianism and monetarism. Keynesianism came up against the harsh reality that stimulating the domestic economy provoked inflation in large measure because the multiplier effect leaked into import demand and created balance-of-payment problems. Monetarists could not control the money supply since the dollar had de facto become the world medium of exchange.

Economic management Japanese-style is a better version of the supply-side thinking that emerged in America in the 1980s. Whereas the American supply-siders merely threw money at problems—lowered taxes for the rich with the hope that productive investment would follow and were disappointed by the speculative fever that was unleashed—Japanese administrative guidance channeled resources into productive growth. While the far more equal income distribution in Japan shows that high growth can be carried on with a far higher degree of equity than has been the case in the United States, and that the sort of gross income differentials and incentives Americans accept as necessary are in fact not common elsewhere, the Japanese system has its own shortcomings. These involve the pursuit of growth above other important quality-of-life goals and a forced conformity that we would not want to adopt. In the 1980s the Japanese also allowed speculative excesses of their bubble economy to endanger stability. What we have to learn from Japan is not some formula that can be swallowed whole.

Urban policy must be seen as part of a national economic development program. Just as Japan and other developmentalist states have had government-led programs to make the most of their people resources, so the United States needs to change its ways. We cannot afford to write off our cities and the majority of their inhabitants. We need to invest in our environment and human resources. Our urban decay is not unrelated to our larger economic difficulties. As we learn more about Japan, we may find that they still have some of the same lessons to master.

Citizens in all the nations of the world, including Japan and the United States, not only have to "Think globally and act locally," as the bumper-sticker slogan would have it; but we have to think globally and act globally to set the terms on which it is possible to create a positive framework in which to act locally. Such a step forward would help the Japanese as well as the United States. The task is daunting. Ordinary people do not act globally. For the most part we think and act only where we are at that moment in time. We make demands on government. The context in which we see the world and understand what the constraints on government activity really are, however, is crucial. The argument here is that the limits we have imposed on government are too narrow, not too broad, as many in the 1980s suggested. Big Government is a problem only when the state is not responsive to democratically determined needs conceived in a long-term inclusive perspective. The understanding of these needs has, in my view, been manipulated. Americans are being told to accept a smaller role of government at a time when a more mature state role is required. The fear of uncontrollably expanding obligations of government is a real one to Americans whose incomes are not keeping up with their personal needs. To meet the obligations to our most needy, and to provide a civilized public space for us all, economic growth is necessary. The pattern of growth is important. Wealth accumulation for the upper 20 percent of the income distribution geared to transnational capital will not, as it has not, trickle down to the majority of Americans who are excluded from benefits. The introduction of an industrial policy (whether or not some new term is put forward for the concept, which resonates with decision makers and the electorate) does not come without some dangers. The form that is selected for the industrial policy and the manner in which it is implemented may intensify the trends toward uneven spatial development that are already evident and heighten the income inequalities between highly paid knowledgeable workers and the majority of the working class. These developments would continue the dangerous pattern of divisiveness that we have discussed.

The U.S.-based transnationals that continue to hold their own in world markets by producing more and more outside of the United States play tax jurisdictions off against each other. The political response to the effects of these activities encourages taxpayer rebellion, which undermines the social fabric and stability of our cities and the nation as a whole. Given the nature of a competitive system, it is unrealistic to think transnationals will change their behavior without a great deal of administrative guidance by national and international regulators who understand the nature of social costs and the dynamics of sustainable growth. The articulate and affluent strata that see their interests cojoined with the international corporate elite are likely to be torn between a desire to do the right thing and a more narrow interpretation of their own self-interest. The problem is, of course, that the leverage of corporate elites will be evermore substantial with regard to distant bureaucrats, unless there is a powerful citizens' movement with awareness of what is at stake for their local community's and their nation's future.

The Japanese challenge offers an opportunity to think about why America seems to be falling apart—not simply our cities but our economy, as well. It is possible that things may in fact not be as bad as they look. The country is in a long recession as this is written. Cyclical recovery, however, will hardly lead to better times for many citizens. To the extent that an expansion is built on high-tech enclaves far from our older city centers, inequalities will grow. The country may be faced with a historic change. Either we act to reconstitute the nation, incorporating those who have been pushed out of the possibility of a productive relationship with the new knowledge-intensive world we are moving into, or the nation faces decline no matter how rich the upper 20 percent or so of us become. Indeed "us" is a more difficult concept as the inclusive America gives way to feuding political divisions.

The urban fiscal crisis must be seen in this broad global context. The policies of the 1980s dramatically increased income inequalities in the United States, redistributed wealth from the poor and middle class to the rich, and shifted much of our social support system from the public sector to the private sector. The structural deficit of $200 billion that the Reagan tax cuts built in to the American fiscal reality puts a constant downward pressure on public spending. Since we must now rely on individual and local government initiatives, the federal government is free to cut revenue sharing, anti-poverty programs, aid to education, and infrastructure spending. The free market response to making America more competitive was to abrogate responsibility in the social realm to the market. The debris from that whirlwind is now falling on us. Such an argument is more than a political denunciation of a partisan sort. Indeed, the Democrats have hardly distinguished themselves with any alternative vision. Rather, my approach has been to ground urban fiscal problems in the larger political economy and to show the manner in which the urban fiscal crisis is a derived crisis. That is, this crisis is a result of larger shifts in the material base of the economy and of the dominant ideology or public philosophy dominant in our decision making. I have stressed the contrast between the United States and a somewhat idealized version of the Japanese approach to make the point that the American way has not met the market test over the past decade and a half, and that we do have alternatives.[11]

Conclusions

The tax bases of our older cities and now most of our states have eroded, and after more than a decade of "Get Big Government Off Our Backs," "Read My Lips," and "Competitive Federalism," the human costs of these policies are clear enough. The country would benefit by simply reversing the policies of the 1980s: restoring the progressivity to the tax system, reinstituting federal revenue sharing, and having the national government once again assume responsibility for social and economic problems that are national in scope and cannot be adequately addressed at the local level. The nation has successfully executed major swings from the free market laissez faire to a mixed economy in which government plays a significant role. There was the redistribution upward in the 1920s and the swing back to the New Deal liberalism of the 1930s, and a second swing to the right with the Eisenhower business-as-usual of the 1950s and a return swing with the New Frontier and Great Society decade of Kennedy and LBJ. After our twelve-year experiment with conservative policies, a similar long swing to the left seems about due. The complication is the extent to which our economy has internationalized and the divisive lack of consensus over how to theorize economic and social policy in this new context.

I would like to conclude by stressing that current efforts to make government more efficient by asking the public sector to run more like a streamlined business are, in the context of the current fiscal crisis of the state and the stagnant macroeconomy, a misplaced emphasis. What they ignore is the basic concern of government—providing high-quality services efficiently. The main task of the present moment is to upgrade the public sector's capacity to provide quality human resource development and physical infrastructure. Only the state can provide these basic services and goods on the scale that the nation needs. These are truly "public goods" with important externalities. The private market cannot be left to decide how much and in what ways they should be provided. A uniformly high level of provision is essential in a modern, democratic society. The problem with contracting out, privatization, and other rationalizations of service provision, which are offered to drive down wages and cost of governance, is that they also deplete the competence of the public sector. Instead, we should be building governmental capacity and paying wages that will attract and hold a competent work-force. To do otherwise is false economy.

The same logic applies to efforts to have jurisdictions compete with each other. It would be to everyone's advantage, including the business community, to harmonize taxation and public policies so that uniform basic service levels can be provided everywhere. Standardizing incentives for industrial development would halt the erosion of local tax bases and provide a consistent known base for business firms. It would be far better for states to move toward a common tax philosophy, uniform sales tax base and rates, than to introduce competition, where competition is likely to generate more costs to society than it is to yield benefits. Better service provision can come from higher-quality management and better trained and motivated workers. After decades of neglect under the supposition that what happens in the government sector is irrelevant to the real action, there is a drive for economy in the public realm. "Cutback economics" is a manifestation of a more general austerity and an effort to shift resources away from meeting public needs. Very rarely are the people who push for economies and efficiency in government the same people who are interested in restoring progressive forms of taxation to fund public services.

What are the obligations of government? The answer depends on whose government it is and how the politically active view the nature of the state. Increasingly, the market-driven inequality that has characterized our economy in recent years has led to a demand to limit government out of a fear that the inadequate income we have will be taxed away and spent on people whom government cannot really help. This fear creates a "lifeboat ethic" in America. The alternative is to redesign urban programs and social policy so that all of our citizens are reincorporated into a productive relation to the larger society, create an inclusive economy by structuring corporate and individual incentives to that end, and adopt some form of industrial policy that meets our unique national interests. The costs of not doing so are unimaginably great.

Notes

1. The implication of this new orientation for cities and regions was to reverse the policies of the previous three decades. As Swartz and Peck (1990a) have written:

> What has been a clear and forthright policy to reduce vertical and horizontal fiscal imbalances among federal, state, and local governments has given way to the establishment of a new "competitive federalism" where governments are expected to finance their own activities . . . if a service cannot be paid for at the level where provided, then do without it.

2. Terry Nichols Clark (1983) sees and approves of a new breed of mayors, the New Fiscal Populists. Unlike traditional Republican leaders like Ronald Reagan and George Bush, who tend to reduce taxes and cut back social programs, or New Deal Democrats who look for new sources of revenue to continue past programs, Clark's NFP-types seek to reduce taxes, but their concern for the disadvantaged leads them to seek ways to maintain services. Contracting out and other efficiency-seeking measures characterize the NFPs.
3. This computer model, which did not restrict policy choice to positive programs and so allowed the computer to raise city per capita income by choosing policies for getting rid of the poor, anticipated the dominant thrust of much of later urban policy.
4. For a summary and explanation of the data sympathetic to Rubin, see Albelda and MacEwan, 1992.
5. Dr. Frederick K. Goodwin, the Bush administration's top mental health official, for example, expressed the view before the Advisory Council of the National Institutes of Mental Health that:

> If you look, for example, at male monkeys, especially in the wild, roughly half of them survive to adulthood. The other half die by violence. That is the natural way it is for males, to knock each other off and, in fact, there are many interesting evolutionary implications of that because the same hyperaggressive monkeys who kill each other are also hypersexual, so they copulate more and therefore they reproduce more to offset the fact that half of them are dying.
>
> Now, one could say that some of the loss of social structure in this society, and particularly within the high impact inner-city areas, has removed some of the civilizing evolutionary things that we have built up and that maybe it isn't just the careless use of the word when people call certain areas in certain cities jungles, that we may have

gone back to what might be more natural, without all of the social controls that we have imposed upon ourselves as a civilization over thousands of years in our own evolution.

This just reminds us that although we look at individual factors and we look at biological differences and we look at genetic differences, the loss of structure in society is probably why we are dealing with this issue. (Hilts 1992, 6.)

6. "State budget cuts aimed at the poorest of the poor were so extensive in 1991 and loom so large next year that states seem to be 'competing to make themselves unattractive places for the poor to live,' says Steven Gold, director of the Center for the Study of the States, a nonpartisan research organization . . . " (Taylor 1991, 32). Also see Persky, Sclar, and Wiewel 1992.

7. *The New Testament,* Matthew 25:31–46.

8. Cited in Johnson 1984.

9. There are, of course, many good studies available. An introduction is Bernard Eccleston, *State and Society in Post-War Japan* (New York: Basil Blackwell, 1989).

10. Michael Porter, *The Competitive Advantage of Nations* (New York: Free Press, 1990).

11. There are, of course, many other ways to make these arguments. It seems to me that progressive urbanists have a good grasp on the causes of urban decline and the present fiscal crisis of many of our large cities (and most of our state governments, as well) and approaches to changing things for the better. What they lack is power to sufficiently influence the course of real world events. Some of the recent literature that is particularly helpful includes:

Allen J. Scott, *Metropolis: From the Division of Labor to Urban Form* (University of California Press, 1988); Mike Davis, *City of Quartz* (Verso, 1990); Gregory D. Squires, editor, *Unequal Partnerships* (Rutgers University Press, 1989); John Forester, *Planning in the Face of Power* (University of California Press, 1989); Naomi Carmon, editor, *Neighborhood Policies and Programmes* (New York: St. Martin's Press, 1990); and Joseph Persky, Elliott Sclar, and Wim Wiewel, *Does America Need Cities? An Urban Investment Strategy for National Prosperity* (Economic Policy Institute, 1991).

References

Albelda, Randy, and MacEwan, Arthur. 1992. "The State of the States: Fiscal Crisis in the 1990s." Union for Radical Political Economics, Allied Social Sciences Meetings, January.

Aschauer, David. 1989. "Is Public Expenditure Productive?" *Journal of Monetary Economics* (March): 177–200.

Bahl, Roy, and Sjoquist, David L. 1990. "The State and Local Fiscal Outlook: What Have We Learned and Where Are We Headed?" *National Tax Journal* (September): 325.

Bradbury, Katharine L.; Downs, Anthony; and Small, Kenneth A. 1981. *Futures for a Declining City: Simulations for the Cleveland Area*. New York: Academic Press.

Clark, Terry Nichols, and Ferguson, Lorna Crowley. 1983. *City Money: Political Processes, Fiscal Strain, and Retrenchment*. New York: Columbia University Press.

Dilger, Robert J., ed. 1986. *American Intergovernmental Relations Today*. New York: Prentice Hall.

Downs, Anthony. 1985. "The Future of Industrial Cities." In Peterson, ed., *The New Urban Reality*, 289.

Drucker, Peter. 1991. "The New Productivity Challenge." *Harvard Business Review* (November–December: 69–79.

Edsall, Thomas Bryne. 1992. "Willie Horton's Message." *New York Review of Books* (February 13): 7.

Edsall, Thomas Bryne, and Edsall, Mary D. 1991. *Chain Reaction: The Impact of Race, Rights and Taxes on American Politics*. New York: W.W. Norton.

Forrester, Jay W. 1969. *Urban Dynamics*. Cambridge, Mass.: MIT Press.

Getler, Michael. 1991. "Once Again, America Faces Japan and Germany." *Washington Post National Weekly Edition* (December 30): 22.

Hilts, Philip J. 1992. "Federal Official Apologizes for Remarks on Inner Cities." *New York Times* (February 22): 6.

Johnson, Chalmers. 1984. "The Industrial Policy Debate Re-examined." *California Management Review* (Fall): 71–9.

———. 1987. "How to Think About Competition from Japan." *Journal of Japanese Studies* 13(2): 422.

Ladd, Helen F. 1990. "Big City Finances in the New Era of Fiscal Federalism." In Swartz and Peck, eds., *The Changing Face of Fiscal Federalism*.

Levine, Harry G. 1991. Keynote Address to the Princeton University Working Group on the Future of Drug Use and Alternatives to Drug Prohibition. Princeton University, December 14: 13.

Magdoff, Harry. 1992. "Globalization—To What End, Part I." *Monthly Review* (February): 7.

Mullen, John K. 1990. "Property Tax Exemptions and Local Fiscal Stress." *National Tax Journal* (December): 467–79.

Munnell, Alicia. 1990. "Why Has Productivity Growth Declined? Productivity and Public Investment." *New England Economic Review* (January–February) 3–22.

Muwakkil, Salim. 1992. "With Jackson Out, Black Vote Uncertain." *In These Times* (February 19–25): 2.

Okun, Arthur. 1975. *Equality and Efficiency*. Washington, D.C.: Brookings Institution.

National Resources Committee, Urban Committee. 1937. *Our Cities, Their Role in the National Economy*. Washington, D.C.: General Printing Office.

Persky, Joseph; Sclar, Eliott; and Wiewel, Wim. 1992. *Does America Need Cities? An Urban Investment Strategy for National Prosperity*. Economic Policy Institute. Washington, D.C.: Economic Policy Institute.

Peterson, Paul E. 1985. "Introduction: Technology, Race, and Urban Policy." In Peterson, ed., *The New Urban Reality*, 1.

——, ed. 1985. *The New Urban Reality*. Washington, D.C.: Brookings Institution.

Phillips, Kevin. 1991. *The Politics of the Rich and Poor: Wealth and the Electorate in the Reagan Aftermath*. New York: Harper Perennial.

Reich, Robert B. 1992. *The Work of Nations: Preparing Ourselves for 21st-Century Capitalism*. New York: Vintage Books.

Rubin, Laura S. 1990. "The Current Fiscal Situation in State and Local Governments." *Federal Reserve Bulletin* (December): 1009–18.

Shannon, John. 1986. "Federal and State-Local Spenders Go Their Separate Ways." In Dilger, ed., *American Intergovernmental Relations Today*.

Sullivan, David F. 1991. "State and Local Government Fiscal Position in 1990." *Survey of Current Business* (February): 31–4.

Swartz, Thomas R., and Peck, John E. 1990. "Six Profiles of the Changing Face of Fiscal Federalism: An Overview." In Swartz and Peck, eds., *The Changing Face of Fiscal Federalism*, 3.

——, eds. 1990. *The Changing Face of Fiscal Federalism*. Armonk, N.Y.: M.E. Sharpe.

Taylor, Paul. 1991. "A Meaner, Harsher Nation." *Washington Post National Weekly Edition* (December 30): 32.

Ueno, Hiroya. 1983. "Industrial Policy: Its Role and Limits." *Journal of Japanese Trade and Industry* (July–August): 34.

7

The City of Detroit:
A Personal Perspective

FRANK J. BONELLO

Introduction

The city of Detroit has been mentioned a number of times in the preceding chapters, and the references are all negative. Professor Lyall reports that Detroit lost more than 35 percent of its manufacturing base during the 1970s. Professor Netzer notes that between 1966 and 1988 Detroit experienced a 64 percent decline in the market value of its real property, a 66 percent decline in its taxable property value base, and a 17 percent decline in constant dollar personal income. Professor Follain remarks on the substantial decline in Detroit's population, while Professor Reschovsky informs us that among American cities Detroit's fiscal position is one of the weakest.

Detroit's problems are not just economic in nature, however. Each year around Halloween, national television news programs air stories on Devil's Night, a new and scary Detroit tradition in which random arson breaks out across the city. The urban social pathologies listed by Professor Swartz—AIDs, drugs, poverty, crime, etc.—are all found with a vengeance in Detroit. Even the local pride and joy generated by championships won by Detroit's sports teams is tarnished by the violent acts of hooligan fans.

But was it always this way? To answer this question, I do not need to engage in much historical research, for I was born and raised in Detroit. Each time I return to my hometown and am stunned by its current reality, I am forced to reflect on the difference between what is and what was. The past for me is the 1950s and my teenage years in Detroit. I recall, with nostalgia perhaps, a city that worked, a city safe and growing, a city providing opportunity and hope.

The 1950s

To convey my picture of Detroit in the 1950s, a few personal facts may be helpful. My family lived in the industrial southwest side of the city. My father and his partner owned their own business, a grocery store established during the Great Depression and located on the fringe of the downtown area. In the 1950s we were middle class in almost every sense of that term.

For our family and for our neighborhood, Detroit offered all we wanted from a city. To begin with, public transportation was cheap and efficient. It was a quick fifteen-minute bus trip with one transfer to get from our home to Tiger Stadium (then Briggs Stadium) to watch the Tigers play baseball or the Lions play football. During my freshman and sophomore years at the University of Detroit, I could rely on the public transportation system to get me to those 8 A.M. classes.

Still another fifteen-minute bus trip, this time without the transfer, would take me to the center of the city with its great department stores—Hudson's and Crowley's, to mention just two—and its cluster of five or six first-run movie theaters. The downtown area was alive. During the day the streets were crowded with people—people who worked in the offices, people who shopped the stores, and people like me who just wanted to experience the dynamic city center. At night, especially weekend nights, people filled the streets in search of entertainment. Downtown to me was always a place of wonder—so many people, so many stores, so many things to do. It was also a place of mystery—just what kind of jobs did the people have, what really went on in all those office buildings, and how did all those goods get into all those stores?

The essence of Detroit, however, was its industrial muscle; it proudly and correctly proclaimed itself the "Motor Car Capital of the World" or, more simply, "The Motor City." Back in the 1950s the only foreign car to be seen (and laughed at) was an import from Germany, the Volkswagen Beetle, and the sightings did not occur very often. It didn't take much to document the importance of automobiles to Detroit; all I had to do was walk down to the busy street at the end of the block, and I could see trucks transporting automobile bodies, engines, other parts, and finished assemblies. Within a five- or six-mile radius of our home there were any number of automobile factories—a Fisher body plant, the Cadillac final assembly plant, and Ford's huge Rouge complex. These were complemented by other factories supporting the automobile industry, including the steel mills on Zug Island, chemical plants, truck and train shipping yards, and so on. These plants produced two things: goods and jobs. It was the jobs that were most important to Detroit and its people. The work was hard, but the pay was good. (I would find this out firsthand with summer jobs as a coke plant laborer on Zug Island and as an inspector in a plant at the Rouge complex.) Back then there were lots of jobs, skilled and unskilled, that allowed people to achieve a middle-class status, jobs that generated sufficient income for families to purchase their own homes, to buy a new car every few years, and to educate their children. The drudgery, monotony, and physical strain of the tough jobs were acceptable on those terms.

What really helped Detroit function effectively during the 1950s was the vitality of its neighborhoods, areas that provided schools, shopping, and recreation. In my neighborhood, a fifteen-minute walk would take me past three second-run movie theaters, theaters that allowed kids to dream away Saturday afternoons and parents to escape the stress and strain of jobs. The stores were a cut below the downtown department stores but provided the wherewithal to satisfy everyday needs. The parks gave us green space, baseball fields, picnic areas, and even some tennis courts. Schools weren't just for education—we exploited their playgrounds; the games back then were baseball, a version of stickball, and football.

There was an ethnic and racial diversity among the neighborhoods. It just seemed logical back then for there to be a Polish neighborhood, a Greek neighborhood, a Hispanic neighborhood, a black neighborhood, and even a neighborhood occupied primarily by people who had just moved to Detroit from the southern part of the country in search of better-paying jobs. Only later would questions arise as to why nonwhite neighborhoods were less attractive and the people poorer.

People in the neighborhoods took pride in their ethnic or racial commonalities; they shopped at the same stores, went to the same movie theaters and saw the same movies, had similar jobs, and sent their children to the same schools. The schools were part of the neighborhood, close to the people. There were three public elementary schools within six blocks of our home and two public high schools within a mile. Almost all the kids walked to school, and bus transportation, for the few who needed it, was on the public transportation system. The yellow school bus seen everywhere today was almost never seen in the Detroit of the 1950s; it was used only in rural areas (and by some of the private schools that operated within the city).

In a real sense then the neighborhood dominated city life. From close ethnic and racial ties to nearby schools, shopping, parks, churches, and even jobs, the neighborhood provided almost everything that people needed. It was possible to live and live well without a car—or even public transportation, for that matter—since the neighborhood offered its residents all the goods and services they needed, as well as good jobs that could support a middle-class lifestyle. People had a vested interest in their neighborhoods; they were the environment in which they lived, in which they raised their children, and they were the site of their largest investment—their owner-occupied homes. Success was measured by one's ability to return to the neighborhood to start a family.

So for a middle-class teenager, Detroit was a good place to live during the 1950s. Even for those who weren't white or middle class, circumstances were not perceived as desperate; at least there was hope. Hope took the form of the real possibility of obtaining a low-skill but good-paying job in one of the city's many thriving industrial plants.

The Beginning of Decline

What happened to transform Detroit from a dynamic industrial power in the 1950s to its current reality? Let me begin by admitting that the Detroit of the 1950s was far from perfect. Even then the poor were concentrated in housing projects; there were episodes of high unemployment as the national economy fell into recession; and occasional racial tensions and racial violence were not uncommon; and people worried that Detroit's economy was too dependent on a single industry. I suspect that if we had looked hard enough back then, we could have found signs of future problems, but we would have been forced to stretch our imaginations beyond the most pessimistic limits to conjure up a vision that replicates the reality of Detroit in 1992.

I will not attempt to outline all the forces that have worked to bring Detroit to its present situation. Let me instead maintain my personal perspective by relating what happened to my father's business and my family's home.

As I have indicated, my father's business, a grocery store, was located on the fringe of downtown, an area of homes, some apartment buildings, and a few other small businesses. The area was not as nice as it had once been, and, compared to other areas located farther away from downtown, it was not prosperous and seemed rather run down. In the early 1960s this area was selected as one of Detroit's first urban renewal sites; that is, the homes, apartments, and businesses were torn down and replaced by new small businesses. The idea behind the Corktown Project, as it was called, was to create new economic activity that would contain urban decay and preserve adjacent areas. My father's grocery store was replaced by a small medical office. Given that my father was near retirement, this dislocation caused no major economic hardship for us. But it did for others. When our grocery store closed, those who lived in the surrounding area were no longer able to walk to a store to buy basic necessities. They now had to drive or catch a bus. This housing stock became less attractive and less marketable. For the people whose homes were torn down and who could afford to, the question was where to relocate. Some of the more affluent chose the suburbs. The less fortunate were forced to relocate to the weakest of the remaining neighborhoods in Detroit. This placed an additional burden on those neighborhoods that were least able to support a large influx of poor people in search of housing. This caused a further deterioration in the quality of life in those neighborhoods. The final insult added to these injuries was that the city had difficulty finding buyers for the new, light industry sites, and redevelopment could at best be described as slow.

As for our home, it too was torn down; the reason—to make room for a new freeway, I–75. That particular project had enormous negative externalities for our neighborhood. The freeway dislocated twenty to forty families on each block in its path. This reduced the economic and population base that supported the neighborhood theaters, stores, schools, and churches. Taxable residential property was replaced by publicly owned strips of concrete that did not yield tax revenue for the city. The freeway also created a clearly identifiable physical barrier six lanes wide between a white middle-class area and a lower-income poorer, nonwhite area; it was much more difficult to cross a six-lane freeway than a busy surface street. Finally, the freeway made it easier for people to move to the suburbs and commute to the city for employment purposes. Over time, with the development of suburban shopping malls and industrial parks, there was less and less incentive to return to the city. Even my family chose not to relocate within the city; we too moved to the suburbs.

Concluding Comments

These two events took place early in the 1960s. In retrospect, it is easy to see that two projects designed to help people—urban renewal and the interstate highway construction program—may have contributed to Detroit's decline, as well as the decline of other older, industrial cities. The decline of a city like Detroit, however, cannot be traced to one or two isolated causes. The complex reality reveals that Detroit's decline was due to a whole set of forces, political and nonpolitical; internal and external; economic and noneconomic; local, national, and international. The crushing blow for Detroit may have been the globalization of the automobile industry and the resulting loss of jobs. Still, with a better understanding of the consequences of public policy actions and a greater appreciation of the nature of economic change, perhaps Detroit's decline could have been cushioned if not arrested. Maybe things could have been different; maybe, just maybe, my present visits to my hometown could have been occasions of pride rather than occasions of despair.

The intention of this book is to promote such understanding and appreciation. Although its title is *Urban Finance Under Siege*, we must remember that people have always constituted the essence of any urban area. If urban finance is under siege, then the people who live in the urban areas are also under siege. That is the reason we cannot ignore the economic conditions of the cities or overlook long-run developing trends. Only with such understanding are we likely to shape proper policies to reverse conditions in the ailing cities and maintain the prosperity of those cities that are fortunate enough to be in good health. This volume, we hope, generates such knowledge.

Index

Contributors

FRANK J. BONELLO is an associate professor of economics and college fellow for the College of Arts and Letters at the University of Notre Dame. He holds B.S. and M.A. degrees from the University of Detroit and a Ph.D. from Michigan State University. He has served as a consultant to the U.S. Air Force and the U.S. Agency for International Development and is currently serving on the Social Science Advisory Board for *World Book Encyclopedia.* He has authored, coauthored, or coedited five books; the sixth edition of *Taking Sides: Clashing Views on Controversial Economic Issues,* coedited with Thomas R. Swartz, was published in early 1993. He has also authored or coauthored more than twenty professional articles and delivered more than twenty papers at professional conferences across the country.

JAMES R. FOLLAIN is a professor of economics and chairman of the Economics Department at Syracuse University. He received his Ph.D. in economics from the University of California at Davis in 1976 and was a senior research associate at the Urban Institute from 1976 to 1979. He also served as an economist with the Federal Home Loan Bank of San Francisco from 1979 to 1980. He served as a professor of finance and director of the Office of Real Estate Research at the University of Illinois from 1984 to 1988 and returned to Syracuse University to head the Economics Department in September 1988. Professor Follain has received a research award from the National Science Foundation and served as a consultant to the World Bank, the U.S.

Department of Housing and Urban Development, the U.S. Agency for International Development, the Office of the Comptroller of the Currency, the Federal Home Loan Bank Board, and other public and private organizations. He served as the president of the American Real Estate and Urban Economics Association in 1989. He serves on the board of editors of the *Journal of Urban Economics,* the *Journal of Housing Economics,* and the *Journal of the American Real Estate and Urban Economics Association.* He is also a member of the Federal National Mortgage Association's Housing Policy Advisory Committee. His current interests include the pricing of debt securities with options, the use of futures contracts to hedge interest rate risk, the impact of tax reform on investment in the real estate market, the demand for adjustable-rate mortgages, and fundamental housing market analysis.

KATHARINE C. LYALL is president of the University of Wisconsin System. Her initial appointment at Wisconsin as vice president for academic affairs began on December 1, 1981. She also served as executive vice president and as acting president for two terms. She holds a professorship in the Department of Economics at the University of Wisconsin–Madison.

A native of Lancaster, Pennsylvania, Lyall received her Ph.D. in economics from Cornell University in 1969 and holds an M.B.A. degree from New York University. Prior to coming to Wisconsin, she served on the research staff of the Chase Manhattan Bank, on the faculty of the Department of Economics at the Maxwell School at Syracuse University, as executive director of the Committee on Evaluation Research for the Russell Sage Foundation, as deputy assistant secretary for economic affairs at the U.S. Department of Housing and Urban Development, and as professor of political economy and director of the Graduate Program in Public Policy at Johns Hopkins University. She has authored numerous books and articles in the fields of public finance, economic development, policy analysis, and evaluation research.

DICK NETZER is a senior fellow in the Urban Research Center and a professor of economics and public administration at New York University. He has been at NYU since 1961, with service as chairman of the Economics Department, dean of the Graduate School of Public Administration, and founding director of the Urban Research Center. His undergraduate education was at the University of Wisconsin, and he received masters degrees and a Ph.D. from Harvard. He has written extensively on public finance, urban economics, and the economics and financing of the arts. He has been an active participant in public affairs as a member of numerous boards and commissions, including a term as a member of the Municipal Securities Rulemaking Board and service as a director of the Municipal Assistance Corporation for the City of New York since the New York City fiscal crisis of 1975. For fifteen years, from 1973 to 1988, he was editor of the quarterly journal *New York Affairs,* and he has served on the editorial boards of a number of other journals, including the *National Tax Journal, Journal of Urban Economics,* and *Public Finance Quarterly.* From 1968 to 1979, he chaired the Inter-University Committee on Urban Economics, a Ford Foundation–sponsored group organized to foster research in this field. He is a member of the American Institute of Certified Planners.

ANDREW RESCHOVSKY is a professor of agricultural economics and public affairs at the University of Wisconsin–Madison. He has a Ph.D. in economics from the University of Pennsylvania and has held previous academic positions at Rutgers University and Tufts University. In addition he has been a consultant to a number of state and local governments throughout the country. His research is primarily in the area of state and local public finance. He has written numerous articles in professional journals and is the principal author of *State Tax Policy: Evaluating the Issues.* He is currently conducting research on long-term tax burdens on the poor and on state aid to local governments.

THOMAS R. SWARTZ is a professor of economics at the University of Notre Dame. He came to South Bend in 1965 after completing degrees at Indiana (Ph.D. 1965), Ohio (M.A. 1962), and LaSalle (B.A. 1960). He has served as a fiscal consultant with federal agencies, the state of Indiana, and a number of local governments. He has authored, coauthored, or coedited four books, three monographs, and more than twenty-five chapters of books or professional articles and delivered more than thirty papers here and abroad. The sixth edition of *Taking Sides: Clashing Views on Controversial Economic Issues,* coedited with Frank J. Bonello, was published in early 1993.

WILLIAM K. TABB is professor of economics and sociology at Queens College, City University of New York. He received his undergraduate degree from Earlham College and his Ph.D. from the University of Wisconsin. He has held a number of visiting teaching positions: State University of New York at Stony Brook, New School for Social Research, University of California at Berkeley, and University of Oregon. He has also been a visiting researcher at Kansai University in Osaka, Japan. He has authored, coauthored, or coedited six books. In addition he has published a number of articles in professional journals and chapters of books. His teaching interests include urban political economy and government and industry, and his research interests focus on urban and regional restructuring and the internationalization of labor and capital.